Ladders to Success on the State Exam

WRITING, HIGH SCHOOL

Ladders to Success on the State Exam, Writing, High School
281NA
ISBN-10: 1-60471-120-5
ISBN-13: 978-1-60471-120-2

Writer: Kimberly Kaufmann
Cover Image: Cover illustration by Mark Collins/Deborah Wolfe Ltd.

Triumph Learning® 136 Madison Avenue, 7th Floor, New York, NY 10016
Kevin McAliley, President and Chief Executive Officer

Printed in the United States of America

10 9 8 7 6 5 4 3 2 1

Ladders to Success on the State Exam

WRITING, HIGH SCHOOL

Table of Contents

Diagnostic Test

PART 1: Revising and Editing

DIRECTIONS
Read the following passages and answer the questions that follow. Remember that you are NOT permitted to use dictionaries or other reference materials on this section of the test.

adapted and excerpted from

The Lost Prince

by Frances Hodgson Burnett

(1) They were not rich enough to buy many books. (2) Loristan knew the treasures of all great cities, the resources of the smallest towns. (3) Together he and his boy walked through the endless galleries filled with the wonders of the world, the pictures before which through centuries an unbroken procession of almost worshiping eyes had passed uplifted. (4) Because his father made the pictures seem the glowing, burning work of still-living men whom the centuries could not turn to dust, because he could tell the stories of their living and laboring to triumph, stories of what they felt and suffered and were, the boy became as familiar with the old masters—Italian, German, French, Dutch, English, Spanish—as he was with most of the countries they had lived in. (5) They were not merely old masters to him, but men who were grate, men who seemed to him to have weelded beautiful swords and held high, splendid lights. (6) His father could not go often with him, but he always took him for the first time to the galleries, museums, libraries, and historical places which were richest in treasures of art, beauty, or story. (7) In time, he knew exactly the places where the great painters hung he knew whether this masterpiece or that was in Vienna, in Paris, in Venice, or Munich, or Rome. (8) He knew stories of splendid crown jewels, of old armor, of ancient crafts, and of roman relics dug up from beneath the foundations of old German cities. (9) He began when he was a very little fellow to make a sort of game out of his rambles through picture-galleries, having no playmates and nothing to play with. (10) Quiet and orderly as he were, he often found himself stared at. (11) Sometimes he brought back rough and crude sketches of objects he wished to ask questions about; loristan could always relates to him the full, rich story of the thing he wanted to know.

1. What is the BEST way to combine sentences 1 and 2?

    A. They were not rich enough to buy many books Loristan knew the treasures of all great cities, and also the resources of the smallest towns.

    B. They were not rich enough to buy many book knew the treasures of all great cities, the resources of the smallest towns.

    C. They were not rich enough to buy many books, but Loristan knew the treasures of all great cities, the resources of the smallest towns.

    D. They were not rich enough to buy many books Loristan knew; the treasures of all great cities, the resources of the smallest towns.

2. What is the subject of sentence 3?

    A. Together

    B. he

    C. he and his boy

    D. endless galleries

3. What type of sentence is sentence 4?

    A. simple

    B. compound

    C. complex

    D. compound-complex

4. What words are misspelled in sentence 5?

    A. *merely* and *splendid*

    B. *masters* and *beautiful*

    C. *grate* and *weelded*

    D. Make no change

5. What part of speech is the word *richest* in sentence 6?

    A. noun

    B. verb

    C. adjective

    D. adverb

6. Where should a semicolon be placed in sentence 7?

A. to replace the first comma

B. after *knew*

C. after *places*

D. after *hung*

7. What word should be capitalized in sentence 8?

A. *armor*

B. *ancient*

C. *roman*

D. *cities*

8. How could sentence 9 be rewritten effectively so that it does not begin with the subject of the sentence?

A. He began, having no playmates and nothing to play with, when he was a very little fellow to make a sort of game out of his rambles through picture-galleries.

B. Having no playmates and nothing to play with, he began when he was a very little fellow to make a sort of game out of his rambles through picture-galleries.

C. He was a very little fellow when he began to make a sort of game out of his rambles through picture-galleries, having no playmates and nothing to play with.

D. The sentence does not begin with the subject.

9. Which word should replace *were* in sentence 10?

A. are

B. will be

C. was

D. Make no change.

10. How should sentence 11 be written correctly?

A. Sometimes he brought back rough and crude sketches of objects he wished to ask questions about; Loristan could always relates to him the full, rich story of the thing he wanted to know.

B. Sometimes he brought back rough and crude sketches of objects he wished to ask questions about; Loristan could always related to him the full, rich story of the thing he wanted to knows.

C. Sometimes he brought back rough and crude sketches of objects he wished to ask questions about; Loristan could always relate to him the full, rich story of the thing he wanted to know.

D. Make no change.

Read this passage excerpted and adapted from an address delivered at the Sorbonne, Paris, April 23, 1910.

"Citizenship in a Republic"

by Theodore Roosevelt

(1) Today I shall speak to you on the subject of individual citizenship, the one subject of vital importance to you, my hearers, and to me and my countrymen, because you and we are citizens of great democratic republics. (2) A democratic republic such as each of ours—an effort to realize in its full sense government by, of, and for the people—represents the most gigantic of all possible social experiments. (3) it is also the one fraught with Greatest possibilities for Good and Evil alike. (4) For you and for us the question of the quality of the individul citizen is supreme. (5) Under other forms of government, under the rule of one man or of a very few men, the quality of the rulers.

(6) but with you and with us the case is different. (7) With you here, and with us in my own home, in the long run, success or failure will be conditioned upon the way in which the average man, the average woman, does his or her duty, first in the ordinary, everyday affairs of life, and next in those great occasional crises which call for the heroic virtues. (8) The average citizen must be a good citizen if our republics is to succeed. (9) The stream will not permanently rise higher than the main source the main source of national power and national greatness is found in the average citizenship of the nation. (10) Therefore it behooves us to do our best to see that the standard of the average citizen is kept high. (11) The average cannot be kept high unless the standard of the leaders is very much higher.

11. What type of sentence is sentence 1?

    A. declarative

    B. interrogative

    C. imperative

    D. exclamatory

12. In sentence 2, what part of speech is the word *democratic*?

    A. noun

    B. verb

    C. adjective

    D. adverb

13. How should sentence 3 be written correctly?

    A. It is also the One fraught with greatest possibilities for good and evil alike.

    B. It is also the one fraught with greatest possibilities for Good and Evil alike.

    C. It is also the one fraught with greatest possibilities for good and evil alike.

    D. Make no change.

14. What word is misspelled in sentence 4?

    A. *question*

    B. *quality*

    C. *individul*

    D. *supreme*

15. What is the problem with sentence 5?

    A. It has no predicate.

    B. It has no subject.

    C. It is an independent clause.

    D. It is a run-on sentence.

16. Which word should be capitalized in sentence 6?

   A. *but*

   B. *you*

   C. *us*

   D. *different*

17. Which word is NOT an adjective in sentence 7?

   A. great

   B. average

   C. long

   D. you

18. How should sentence 8 be written correctly?

   A. The average citizen must be a good citizen if our republics is to succeed.

   B. The average citizen must be good citizens if our republics are to succeed.

   C. The average citizen must be a good citizen if our republics are to succeed.

   D. Make no change.

19. What is the BEST way to correct sentence 9?

   A. Insert a comma between the two phrases "the main source".

   B. Break the sentence into two between the two phrases "the main source".

   C. Capitalize the word *national* whenever it appears.

   D. Make no change.

20. What is the BEST way to combine sentences 10 and 11?

   A. It behooves us therefore to do our best to see that the standard of the average citizen is kept high until the average cannot be kept high unless the standard of the leaders is very much higher.

   B. Therefore it behooves us to do our best to see that the standard of the average citizen is kept high, the average cannot be kept high unless the standard of the leaders is very much higher.

   C. Therefore it behooves us to do our best to see that the standard of the average citizen is kept high: the average cannot be kept high unless the standard of the leaders is very much higher.

   D. Therefore it behooves us to do our best to see that the standard of the average citizen is kept high, and the average cannot be kept high unless the standard of the leaders is very much higher.

Book Analysis

(1) I resisted reading the novel "Girl with a Bike" for a long time, and I'm not sure why. (2) Avoided the novel because I had built up certain expectations about it. (3) Now i understands it's popularity. (4) The novel is a classic because it develops unique characters, tells an intriguing story, and conveys a Universal theme.

(5) The character is called "girl" in the novel's title, but she is far more than that. (6) Eleanor unfolds for readers as a complicated, fun-loving creature. (7) She enjoys riding bikes, of course, but she is also an expert at crewel embroidery. (8) She plays jokes on a variety of people, including her younger siblings, her grandmother, and the Methodist minister. (9) Eleanor intrigues me because she seems like both a young girl and a wise older woman.

(10) eleanor embarks on an exciting series of events that shape her growing personality. (11) When she volunteers to care for an elderly woman down the street, Eleanor has no idea what she is getting herself into.

(12) I can recommend it as a fine piece of writing without giving the story away. (13) The fascinating Eleanor peppers the story's events with humor and spirit, even while she is learning to value those things in life that cannot be seen. (14) I hope that, like Eleanor, my life will be one wear invisable virtues define me more than anything else.

21. How would you correct sentence 1?

    A. I resisted reading the novel "Girl with a Bike" for a long time I'm not sure why.

    B. I resisted reading the novel *Girl with a Bike* for a long time, and I'm not sure why.

    C. I resisted reading the novel Girl with a Bike for a long time, I'm not sure why.

    D. Make no change.

22. What is the problem with sentence 2?

    A. It has no predicate.

    B. It has no subject.

    C. It is an independent clause.

    D. It is a run-on sentence.

23. How should sentence 3 be written correctly?

    A. Now i understand it is popularity.

    B. Now i understand its popularity.

    C. Now I understand its popularity.

    D. Make no change.

24. What is the BEST way to improve the capitalization in sentence 4?

    A. Uppercase *classic*.

    B. Lowercase *The.*

    C. Capitalize *Novel.*

    D. Lowercase *Universal.*

25. Which word is a noun in sentence 5?

    A. *character*

    B. *is*

    C. *are*

    D. *far*

26. Which of the following suggestions would improve paragraph 2?

 A. Make all the sentences passive.

 B. Vary the sentence beginnings.

 C. Use fewer complicated words.

 D. Combine all the sentences into one.

27. What is the capitalization error in sentence 10?

 A. Capitalize *exciting.*

 B. Capitalize *personality.*

 C. Capitalize *eleanor.*

 D. It is correct as is.

28. What part of sentence 11 is the independent clause?

 A. When she volunteers

 B. to care for an elderly woman

 C. down the street

 D. Eleanor has no idea what she is getting herself into.

29. How could sentence 12 be rewritten so that it does not begin with the subject of the sentence?

 A. I can, without giving the story away, recommend it as a fine piece of writing.

 B. Without giving the story away, I can recommend it as a fine piece of writing.

 C. I can recommend it, without giving the story away, as a fine piece of writing.

 D. It does not begin with the subject.

30. How should sentence 14 be written correctly?

 A. I hope that, like Eleanor, my life will be one where invisible virtues define me more than anything else.

 B. I hope that, like Eleanor, my life will be one where invisable virtues define me more than anything else.

 C. I hope that, like Eleanor, my life will be one were invisible virtues define me more than anything else.

 D. Make no change.

Tropical Rainforests

(1) Discussions of climate change become more common. (2) People are hearing about certain areas of the world which may be most affected by such changes. (3) One such place is the tropical rainforest.

(4) Tropical rainforests develops near the equator because that is where warm and rainy weather can be found. (5) South America, Asia, and Africa contain the largest reign forests but their are also rain forests in North America.

(6) Because the temperature is always warm and always moist the plants in a rainforest are always green. (7) These plants are getting whatever they need, so they continue to grow. (8) A canopy is formed over the rest of the forest by the treetops of the tall trees. (9) The foliage is so thick that only a small portion of the sunshine gets through to the bottom of the forest floor.

(10) But the floor of a tropical rainforest is still teeming with plant and animal life. (11) Vines cling to the lower trunks of trees and climb upward towards the sunlight. (12) Many plants have enormous leaves in order to catch as much light as possible. (13) This enables them to continue growing. (14) Animals in the rainforest. (15) By hideing, they keep themselves safe from other predators. (16) Sloths, snakes, and frogs also call rainforests home. (17) Birds, such as toucans and macaws, savor the fruit that grows plentifully.

31. What is the BEST way to combine sentences 1 and 2?

    A. Discussions of climate change become more common, people are hearing about certain areas of the world which may be most affected by such changes.

    B. Discussions of climate change become more common people are hearing about certain areas of the world which may be most affected by such changes.

    C. As discussions of climate change become more common, people are hearing about certain areas of the world which may be most affected by such changes.

    D. They cannot be combined.

32. Which word makes the subject-verb agreement error in sentence 4?

    A. *rainforests*

    B. *develops*

    C. *is*

    D. *found*

33. How should sentence 5 be written correctly?

    A. South America, Asia, and Africa contain the largest rainforests, but there are also rainforests in North America.

    B. South America, Asia, and Africa contain the largest reignforests but these are also rain forests in North America.

    C. South America, Asia, and Africa contain the largest rainforests but they're are also rainforests in North America.

    D. Make no change.

34. How would you correct sentence 6?

    A. Add a comma after *moist.*

    B. Add a subject to the sentence.

    C. Change the period to a question mark.

    D. Make no change.

35. What type of sentence is sentence 7?

    A. simple

    B. compound

    C. complex

    D. compound-complex

36. What would be the BEST way to improve sentence 8?

    A.   Use simpler words.

    B.   Use the active voice.

    C.   Use more words.

    D.   Use parallel structure.

37. How could sentences 12 and 13 be combined so that the new sentence is NOT a compound sentence?

    A.   Many plants have enormous leaves in order to catch as much light as possible; this enables them to continue growing.

    B.   Many plants have enormous leaves in order to catch as much light as possible, which enables them to continue growing.

    C.   Many plants have enormous leaves in order to catch as much light as possible, this enables them to continue growing.

    D.   Many plants have enormous leaves in order to can catch as much light as possible, and this enables them to continue growing.

38. Which of the following BEST describes sentence 14?

    A.   a simple sentence

    B.   a predicate phrase

    C.   a sentence fragment

    D.   a dependent clause

39. How would you correct sentence 15?

    A.   Change *hideing* to *hiding.*

    B.   Change *keep* to *keeps.*

    C.   Change *themselves* to *themself.*

    D.   Make no change.

40. What part of speech is the word *plentifully* in sentence 17?

    A.   noun

    B.   verb

    C.   adjective

    D.   adverb

Part 2: Writing

Writing Prompt: Narrative Writing

Read the prompt below and write a well-organized composition of at least 250 words. Be sure to follow the suggestions listed under the prompt.

You are writing personal memoirs in your writing class at a community center. The instructor began the class by describing some of her own most frustrating experiences in life. Now she wants you to write a narrative about a frustrating experience of your own. She also wants you to focus on what you learned from the experience.

Before you begin to write, reflect on some of your past frustrations. What specific events led to that frustration? Where did the events take place? Who was involved? What did you learn from the experience?

Now write a multiparagraph composition for your class about what the frustrating experience was and how you learned something from it. Write your composition on the following pages.

- **Remember your audience is the other members of the writing class at the community center; this would include young people as well as local adults.**

- **Include details about characters, setting, plot, and theme.**

- **Be sure to write clearly and to check your composition for correct spelling, punctuation, and grammar.**

Writing Prompt: Persuasive Writing

Read the prompt below and write a well-organized, multiparagraph composition of at least 250 words. Be sure to follow the suggestions listed under the prompt.

The advisor of your school newspaper has invited students to submit articles to the school newspaper. The advisor has asked students to write persuasive essays about how young people can affect their local communities.

Before you begin to write, think about issues within your local community. What changes or improvements need to be made? How can young people participate in those changes or improvements? How will you convince readers to think or act the way you hope they will?

Now write a multiparagraph composition for the advisor about how young people can affect their local communities. Write your composition on the following pages.

- **Remember your audience is the student body of your school; use appropriate language.**

- **Include solid reasoning and appropriate appeal so your readers will respond to your position.**

- **Be sure to write clearly and to check your composition for correct spelling, punctuation, and grammar.**

Writing Prompt: Informational Writing

Read the prompt below and write a well-organized, multiparagraph composition of at least 250 words. Be sure to follow the suggestions listed under the prompt.

In a world history class, you are discussing some of the different historical eras. Your teacher has assigned students to write an essay in which you describe a particular time period that interests you.

Before you begin to write, think about several of the time periods which you know a lot about; for example: ancient Greece, ancient West Africa, colonial America, Civil War America, or World War II. What are some of the features of that time period? What facts and details can you provide to elaborate on your topic?

Now write a multiparagraph composition for your teacher about one of these historical time periods. Write your answer on the following pages.

- **Remember your audience is the other students in your class; use appropriate language.**

- **Include facts and enough information so your readers will understand your explanation.**

- **Be sure to write clearly and to check your composition for correct spelling, punctuation, and grammar.**

Writing Prompt: Literary Writing

Read the poem below and write a well-organized, multiparagraph literary response of at least 250 words. Be sure to follow the suggestions listed under the box.

Solitude

by Ella Wheeler Wilcox

Laugh, and the world laughs with you;
Weep, and you weep alone.
For the sad old earth must borrow its mirth,
But has trouble enough of its own.
Sing, and the hills will answer;
Sigh, it is lost on the air.
The echoes bound to a joyful sound,
But shrink from voicing care.

Rejoice, and men will seek you;
Grieve, and they turn and go.
They want full measure of all your pleasure,
But they do not need your woe.

Be glad, and your friends are many;
Be sad, and you lose them all.
There are none to decline your nectared wine,
But alone you must drink life's gall.

Feast, and your halls are crowded;
Fast, and the world goes by.
Succeed and give, and it helps you live,
But no man can help you die.
There is room in the halls of pleasure
For a long and lordly train,
But one by one we must all file on
Through the narrow aisles of pain.

Now write a multiparagraph literary response about some elements within the poem. For example, you might focus on the theme, the language, or the point of view. Write your answer on the following pages.

- Remember your audience is your literature teacher and your classmates.

- Include specific details from the text and enough information so your readers will understand your interpretation.

- Be sure to write clearly and to check your composition for correct spelling, punctuation, and grammar.

Lesson 1 • Spelling

Correct **spelling** helps a reader understand what has been written. Here are some key rules for correct spelling:

- Put *i* before *e* except after *c* or when sounded as long *a*.
  Examples: *piece, relief; receive, conceive; neighbor, reign*

- If a word ends in *-s, -z, -x, -sh,* or *-ch,* add *-es* to form the plural.
  Examples: *mix, mixes; gas, gases; watch, watches*

- If a word ends in *-f* or *-fe,* change the *f* or *fe* to *v* and add *-es* to form the plural.
  Examples: *leaf, leaves; wife, wives*

- For words that end with a consonant and *y,* change the *y* to *i* and add *-es* to form the plural.
  Examples: *cherry, cherries; folly, follies*

These are some words that are easily misspelled:

Misspelled Words	Correct Spellings
neice	niece
decieve	deceive
lifes	lives
enemys	enemies

Homophones are words that sound like other words but have different meanings and spellings.

Common Homophones	
knew	new
where	wear
which	witch
fourth	forth
break	brake
course	coarse
won	one
weight	wait
its	it's
to	too, two
there	their, they're

DIRECTIONS
Read these sentences. Think will help you answer each question.

(1) Mark Twain new how to turn a phrase. (2) He once wrote, "My own luck has been curious all my literary life; I never could tell a lie that anyone would doubt, nor a truth that anybody would beleive."

1. Which word is NOT used correctly in sentence 1?

A. phrase

B. new

C. turn

D. to

Think

1. **Reread the question. What is it about?**

    Think It is a question about a word not being used correctly.

2. **What must you do to answer the question?**

    Think I must figure out which answer choice contains an incorrectly used word. I must think about how certain words are easily confused with others.

3. **Try out each answer choice.**

    Think The words *phrase*, *new*, and *turn* are all spelled correctly. *Phrase* and *turn* are not usually confused with other words. *New* is often confused with *knew*. In sentence 1, *knew* would be the correct word.

4. **Choose the BEST answer.**

    Think Answer B is the best answer.

2. Which word in sentence 2 is misspelled?

A. curious

B. wrote

C. beleive

D. would

Think

1. **Reread the question. What is it about?**

    Think It is a question about a misspelled word.

2. **What must you do to answer the question?**

    Think I must remember the rules of good spelling.

3. **Try out each answer choice.**

    Think The words *curious* and *wrote* look like they are spelled correctly. *Beleive* has an *i* and *e* together, so I must remember the rules about *i* and *e*. The way *beleive* is spelled here breaks the rule.

4. **Choose the BEST answer.**

    Think Answer C is the best answer.

DIRECTIONS
Read this paragraph. Then circle the best answer to each question below. The hints can help you find the correct answers.

(1) Are you going to Seema's party on the forth? (2) Witch outfit are you planning too where? (3) I can't weight. (4) We can put all our worrys aside and enjoy a fun night.

1. How can you make sentence 1 correct?

   A. Change *going* to *giong*.

   B. Change *party* to *partee*.

   C. Change *forth* to *fourth*.

   D. It is correct as is.

   Hint Is any word in the sentence a homophone?

2. How should sentence 2 be written correctly?

   A. Which outfit are you planning to where?

   B. Which outfit are you planning to wear?

   C. Witch outfit are you planning to wear?

   D. It is correct as is.

   Hint Homophones are words that sound alike but are spelled differently and have different meanings.

3. How would you correct sentence 3?

   A. Change *weight* to *wieght*.

   B. Change *weight* to *wate*.

   C. Change *weight* to *wait*.

   D. It is correct as is.

   Hint What word is a homophone for *weight*? How is it spelled correctly?

4. How should sentence 4 be written correctly?

   A. We can put all our worries aside and enjoy a fun night.

   B. We can put all our worrys aside and enjoy a fun night.

   C. We can put all hour worries aside and enjoy a fun night.

   D. It is correct as is.

   Hint What is the rule for making a word plural if it ends with a consonant and *y*?

5. Rewrite these sentences so that all misspelled words are correct.

Sam cannot concieve of a life without comedians. He loves there storys and is determined too perform stand-up himself won day.

_____

_____

_____

One key spelling rule is if a word has a long *a* sound, the *e* comes before the *i*, as in *weigh*. Other times when *e* comes before *i* are *weird*, *height*, *their*, *foreign*, and *Keith*.

Here are some additional spelling rules:

- When adding *-ly* to a word ending with *-l*, do not drop the *-l*.
  Examples: *real*, *really*; *casual*, *casually*

- Drop a final *e* if an ending or suffix begins with a vowel.
  Examples: *believe*, *believing*; *debate*, *debatable*

- Keep the final *e* if an ending or suffix begins with a consonant.
  Examples: *use*, *useful*; *bore*, *boredom*
  Important exceptions: *judge*, *judgment*; *argue*, *argument*

Here are some other words that are frequently confused with each other.

Commonly Confused Words	
affect (to influence or change)	effect (a result or change)
accept (to receive or agree)	except (all but something)
advice (suggestions)	advise (to provide advice)
were (past tense of "to be")	we're (contraction for "we are")

DIRECTIONS
Read the story. Use the Reading Guide for tips. Then answer the questions on the next page.

The Sweet Smell of Success

(1) Some people think success is just a matter of luck. (2) Others say its a function of hard work. (3) Thomas Edison had his own thoughts on the matter. (4) He said, "Success is 10 percent inspiration and 90 percent perspiration."

(5) In some cases, it can be hard to tell. (6) Take my freind Jamie. (7) She's been on an unbelievable winning streak on her school's tennis team this year. (8) Last year she barely even played, and when she did, she typicaly cracked under the pressure. (9) Now she's dominateing the feild.

(10) Jamie has many theorys on why she's winning all her matchs. (11) She thinks the cool whether is having a positive affect, since she's originaly from a colder climate. (12) She thinks exerciseing at the track is making a big difference. (13) She even thinks its her lucky purple socks. (14) I don't know what to beleive. (15) I just no she never looses!

Reading Guide

What is the mistake in sentence 2?

....

What spelling rule is not followed in sentence 6? How would you correct it?

....

What rule is broken twice in sentence 12? How would you correct the words?

DIRECTIONS
Use the passage on the previous page to answer the questions below. Circle the letter beside the correct answer. The hints can help you find the correct answers.

1. How would you correct sentence 2?

    A. Change *function* to *funtcion*.

    B. Change *its* to *it's*.

    C. Change *others* to *other's*.

    D. It is correct as is.

    Hint Look for a homophone in this sentence.

2. Which word is spelled incorrectly in sentence 8?

    A. typicaly

    B. barely

    C. pressure

    D. cracked

    Hint What is the rule about adding -*ly* when a word ends with *l*?

3. How should sentence 9 be correctly written?

    A. Now she's dominating the feild.

    B. Now she's dominateing the field.

    C. Now she's dominating the field.

    D. It is correct as is.

    Hint What is the rule about the final *e* when an ending begins with a vowel?

4. How would you correctly pluralize the word *theory* in sentence 10?

    A. by adding -*ies*

    B. by dropping the *y* and adding -*es*

    C. by changing the *y* to *i* and adding -*es*

    D. It is correct as is.

    Hint *Theory* ends in a consonant and *y*.

5. On the lines below, rewrite the last paragraph of the passage so that all misspelled words are correct.

    _____

    _____

    _____

    _____

    _____

    _____

    _____

    _____

Step 3

This speech was delivered by Napoleon Bonaparte, Emperor of France, on April 20, 1814, after he was defeated by the Allies and forced to abdicate. Read the speech, and then answer the questions below.

A Somber Goodbye

Napoleon Bonaparte, 1769–1821

(1) Soldeirs of my Old Guard: I bid you farewell. (2) For twenty years I have constantly accompanied you on the road to honor and glory. (3) In these latter times, as in the daze of our prosperity, you have invariably been models of courage and fidelity. (4) With men such as you our cause could not be lost; but the war would have been interminable; it would have been civil war, and that would have entailed deeper misfortunes on France.

(5) I have sacrificed all of my interests to those of the country.

(6) I go, but you, my friends, will continue to serve France. (7) Her happyness was my only thought. (8) It will still be the object of my wishes. (9) Do not regret my fate; if I have consented to survive, it is to serve your glory. (10) I intend to write the history of the great achievments we have performed together. (11) Goodbye, my friends. (12) Would I could press you all to my heart.

Circle the letter of the best answer.

1. Which spelling rule is not followed in sentence 1?

   A. Letter *a* always comes before *u*.

   B. Letter *i* comes before *e* except after *c* and when sounded as long *a*.

   C. A double *l* cannot follow a consonant.

   D. With a final *f*, change the *f* to *v* and add *-es* to form the plural.

2. How should you correct the homophone mistake in sentence 3?

   A. Change *In* to *Inn*.

   B. Change *our* to *hour*.

   C. Change *daze* to *days*.

   D. Change *been* to *Ben*.

3. What is the correct way to write sentence 7?

   A. Her hapiness was my only thought.

   B. Her happiness was my only thought.

   C. Her happines was my only thought.

   D. It is correct as is.

4. Which spelling rule is not followed in sentence 10?

   A. Keep a final *e* if an ending or suffix begins with a consonant.

   B. Drop a final *e* if an ending or suffix begins with a vowel.

   C. Put *i* before *e* except after *c*.

   D. Put *e* before *i* if a word is sounded as a long *a*.

DIRECTIONS
Read the story. Use the Reading Guide for tips that can help you identify misspelled words as you read. Then answer the questions on the next page.

Robots for Everyone

(1) Need some extra help cleaning your room? (2) Some day yore own personal robot might come to the rescue.

(3) Scientists in South Korea recently built a lifelike female android named EveR-1. (4) The robot, which looks like a young Korean woman, can talk and make several facial expressions. (5) With the help of small motors, it can even move it's head, arms, hands, and upper body.

(6) South Korean researchers are developing many types of robot technologys. (7) Some small companys in South Korea already make robots that vacuum and clean houses, according to *National Geographic News.*

(8) But the South Korean government plans to mass produce a new kind of "intelligent" robot, like EveR-1, that can provide many services—including doing chores. (9) In fact, the government would like to put a robot in every home in South Korea by 2020, *National Geographic News* reports.

(10) Oh Sang Rok oversees this new robot project at the South Korean Ministry of Information and Communication.

(11) "Social and economic needs for intelligent service robots to support people's daily lifes are increasing with the advance of an ageing society," Oh told *National Geographic News.*

(12) EveR-1 cannot walk, or even sit. (13) But more advanced androids, and improvments to EveR-1, are in the works.

(14) "We aim to make efforts to develop the robot to be more like humans," Baeg Moon-hong, who created EveR-1, told the *Korea Times.* (15) Baeg, a senior researcher at the Korea Institute of Industrial Technology, said he hopes EveR-1 can walk in the future. (16) So stay on the lookout—a fancier version of EveR-1 may be available four your home one day!

Reading Guide

What word is used incorrectly in sentence 2?

....

One word is used incorrectly in sentence 5. What homophone for this word would be correct?

....

In sentence 6, how would you correctly make *technology* plural?

....

How would you correct sentence 11? What two rules are broken here?

....

Sentence 16 uses one incorrect homophone. What would the correct homophone be?

DIRECTIONS
Now read each question. Circle the letter of the best answer.

1. How should sentence 2 be written correctly?

   A. Some day you're own personal robot might come to the rescue.

   B. Some day your own personal robot might come two the rescue.

   C. Some day your own personall robot might come to the rescue.

   D. Some day your own personal robot might come to the rescue.

   | Hint | Which word is misspelled in the sentence? |

2. In sentence 7, how would you correctly make *company* plural?

   A. Drop the *y* and add *-es*.

   B. Change the *y* to *i* and add *-es*.

   C. Change the *y* to *i* and add *-s*.

   D. It is correct as is.

   | Hint | What is the spelling rule for words that end in a consonant and *y*? |

3. How would you correct the two spelling mistakes in sentence 11?

   A. Change *people's* to *peoples* and *lifes* to *lives*.

   B. Change *increasing* to *increaseing* and *ageing* to *aging*.

   C. Change *daily* to *daley* and *people's* to *peoples*.

   D. Change *lifes* to *lives* and *ageing* to *aging*.

   | Hint | Look at how endings are added to different words. What mistakes do you see? |

4. How would you correctly spell *improvments* in sentence 13?

   A. improvements

   B. improvemants

   C. immmprovments

   D. improvemints

   | Hint | Does the ending attached to this word begin with a vowel or a consonant? |

5. Review sentence 16. Which pair of homophones contains a word used incorrectly in this sentence?

   A. *so* and *sew*

   B. *be* and *bee*

   C. *one* and *won*

   D. *four* and *for*

   | Hint | What is the definition of homophone? |

DIRECTIONS
Read this sample student essay about the writing of Emily Brontë. Then answer the questions on the next page.

A Passion for Words

(1) Emily Brontë had a short but intense life as a writer. (2) Only 30 years old when she died of tuberculosis in 1848, she left behind a stirring body of work, includeing the masterpeice *Wuthering Hieghts*. (3) The novel is an unusualy haunting tale of mystery and doomed love.

(4) Brontë's flare for dramatic language is especially evident in her poetry. (5) In these excerpts from the poem "Stars", Brontë's narrator emphatically pleads with the stars to return after they are banished by the sun's "hostile light." (6) What greif this event has caused!

Stars

(1)   Ah! why, because the dazzleing sun
       Restored our earth to joy
       Have you departed, every one,
       And left a dessert sky?...

(2)   Why did the mourning dawn to brake
       So grate, so pure a spell,
       And scorch with fire the tranquil cheek
       Wear you're cool radiance fell?

(3)   Blood-red he rose, and arrow-straight
       His feirce beams struck my brow:
       The soul of Nature sprang elate,
       But mine sank sad and low!...

(4)   O Stars and Dreams and Gentle Night;
       O Night and Stars return!
       And hide me from the hostile light
       That does not warm, but burn—

(5)   That drains the blood of suffering men;
       Drinks tears, instead of dew:
       Let me sleep threw his blinding riegn,
       And only wake with you!

DIRECTIONS
Read each question. Circle the letter of the best answer.

1. How should the last part of sentence 2 be written correctly?

   A. ...she left behind a stirring body of work, including the masterpeice *Wuthering Heights*.

   B. ...she left behind a stiring body of work, including the masterpiece *Wuthering Heights*.

   C. ...she left behind a stirring body of work, includeing the masterpiece *Wuthering Heights*.

   D. ...she left behind a stirring body of work, including the masterpiece *Wuthering Heights*.

2. How should you correct sentence 3?

   A. Change *tale* to *tail*.

   B. Change *unusualy* to *unusually*.

   C. Change *haunting* to *haunteing*.

   D. Change *doomed* to *domed*.

3. What rule should be used in sentence 6?

   A. Put *e* before *i* if a word is sounded as a long *a*.

   B. Put *i* before *e* except after *c*.

   C. Put *e* before *i* in the words *weird*, *their*, and *foreign*.

   D. The sentence is correct.

4. Which incorrect word is mistaken for a correct word in stanza 1?

   A. sun

   B. to

   C. departed

   D. dessert

5. What rule is not followed in both sentence 2 and stanza 1?

   A. For words ending with a consonant and *y*, change the *y* to *i* and add -*es* to form the plural.

   B. Put *i* before *e* except after *c*.

   C. Drop a final *e* if an ending or suffix begins with a vowel.

   D. Keep a final *e* if an ending or suffix begins with a consonant.

6. How can you correct stanza 3?

   A. Change *feirce* to *fierce*.

   B. Change *sprang* to *spring*.

   C. Change *low* to *lo*.

   D. Change *Blood-red* to *Blood-read*.

7. Which two words in stanza 5 should you change to make the stanza correct?

   A. *blood* and *suffering*

   B. *dew* and *threw*

   C. *suffering* and *blinding*

   D. *threw* and *riegn*

8. On a separate sheet of paper, rewrite stanza 2, fixing all spelling errors. Explain what homophones are, and identify at least three homophones that are used incorrectly in this stanza.

Lesson 2 • Punctuation

Punctuation is the use of marks that help a reader understand the meaning of a sentence. Here are some important punctuation rules:

- End every statement with a period (.), every question with a question mark (?), and every exclamation with an exclamation point (!).

- Place a comma
  after each item on a list.
  after an introductory phrase or subordinate clause.
  to separate two independent clauses joined by the words *and, but, nor, for,* or *yet.*
  to introduce direct quotations.

- Use quotation marks
  at the beginning and end of any lines spoken by people.
  to indicate the titles of articles, poems, songs, short stories, and book chapters.

- Place periods, commas, exclamation points, or question marks before the quotation mark at the end of a quotation.

- Use a semicolon
  to join two sentences when there is not a conjunction.
  before certain joining words like *however* and *nevertheless* when they join two sentences.

- Use a colon
  to separate hours and minutes in time.
  to introduce a list formally.

- Use italics to indicate the titles of books, plays, newspapers, movies, and periodicals.

These are some common punctuation errors.

Punctuation Error	Correct Punctuation
Why did you attend the party, last *night*.	Why did you attend the party last *night?*
"The soup was *delicious*", said Ramon.	"The soup was *delicious*," said Ramon.
I think that my candidate is the best *choice* he believes in many of the same ideas.	I think that my candidate is the best *choice;* he believes in many of the same ideas.

DIRECTIONS
Read these sentences. **Think** will help you answer each question.

(1) I finished my homework assignment I ran to the gym. (2) I burst in and shouted "Here I am!"

1. Where should a semicolon be placed in sentence 1?

    A. between *finished* and *my*

    B. between *homework* and *assignment*

    C. between *assignment* and *I*

    D. after *gym*

Think

1. **Reread the question. What is it about?**

   Think It is a question about where a semicolon should be placed in the sentence.

2. **What must you do to answer the question?**

   Think I must figure out which answer choice contains the correct location. I must think about how a semicolon is used.

3. **Try out each answer choice.**

   Think A semicolon should separate two sentences when there is no conjunction. The first sentence does not end with the word *finished, homework,* or *gym.* The end of the first sentence is the word *assignment.* A semicolon should be placed after that word.

4. **Choose the BEST answer.**

   Think Answer C is the best answer.

2. What punctuation mark should be inserted after the word *shouted*?

    A. comma

    B. exclamation point

    C. question mark

    D. period

Think

1. **Reread the question. What is it about?**

   Think It is a question about a missing punctuation mark.

2. **What must you do to answer the question?**

   Think I must remember the rules of punctuation in quotations.

3. **Try out each answer choice.**

   Think I know that exclamation points, question marks, and periods come at the end of sentences, and this is not the end of the sentence. I also know that a comma is used to introduce direct quotations. A comma is the missing punctuation mark.

4. **Choose the BEST answer.**

   Think Answer A is the best answer.

DIRECTIONS
Read this paragraph. Then circle the best answer to each question below. The hints can help you find the correct answers.

(1) Rosemary is an important herb in Mediterranean cooking? (2) We use it frequently at our house although we do not grow it fresh. (3) The flavor is delicious with meat such as beef or lamb; it is also tasty with roasted potatoes. (4) In fact, I once wrote a poem called Rosemary Is My Friend.

1. How can you make sentence 1 correct?

   A. Add a comma after *herb.*

   B. Change the question mark to a period.

   C. Insert a colon after *Mediterranean.*

   D. It is correct as is.

   Hint   What type of sentence is this?

2. How should sentence 2 be written correctly?

   A. We use it frequently at our house; although we do not grow it fresh.

   B. We use it frequently at our house although we do not "grow it fresh".

   C. We use it frequently at our house, although we do not grow it fresh.

   D. It is correct as is.

   Hint   Subordinate clauses should be separated from independent clauses by a punctuation mark.

3. How would you correct sentence 3?

   A. Change the final period to a question mark.

   B. Insert a comma after *tasty.*

   C. Place a colon after *meat.*

   D. It is correct as is.

   Hint   The sentence contains two independent clauses without a conjunction.

4. How should sentence 4 be written correctly?

   A. In fact, I once wrote a poem called "Rosemary Is My Friend."

   B. In fact I once wrote a poem called: Rosemary Is My Friend.

   C. In fact; I once wrote a poem called Rosemary Is My Friend.

   D. It is correct as is.

   Hint   What is the rule for titles of poems?

5. Rewrite these sentences so that all punctuation is correct.

   One of my favorite books is "A Tale of Two Cities". Have you ever read it. Before I read it I assumed it was a dull book: however the plot is quite exciting.

   _____

   _____

   _____

   _____

Punctuation guides readers to a better understanding of a text. Punctuation directs readers to pause or to think about information in a specific way. For example, a question mark tells the reader that the sentence is asked rather than stated.

Here are some additional punctuation rules:

- Use a hyphen to join two or more words that function as a single word.
- Use a dash
    to emphasize a point.
    to mark a break in thought.
- Place an apostrophe to show ownership.

Here are some other common punctuation errors.

Punctuation Error	Correct Punctuation
The *dogs* bone sat on the table.	The *dog's* bone sat on the table.
Sharon's *selfesteem* suffered after her poor score.	Sharon's *self-esteem* suffered after her poor score.

DIRECTIONS
Read the story. Use the Reading Guide for tips. Then answer the questions on the next page.

Discovering Art

(1) When Samantha visited the National Art Gallery last summer she was astonished. (2) "I would not have believed there could be so many different types of art" she told her friends. (3) She named her favorites; Egyptian art, the Impressionists, and modern sculpture.

(4) As she walked into one of the Impressionist galleries, she gasped. (5) Monets painting looked so real from a distance. (6) She moved closer the painting was simply strokes of color. (7) Pinks, blues, greens—the painting was covered with them.

(8) Nobody was surprised the following fall when Samantha wrote a paper called Monet and Me. (9) Samantha even signed up for a painting class? (10) She may have discovered a future career in the art's.

Reading Guide

What is the mistake in sentence 1?

....

What punctuation rule is not followed in sentence 6? How would you correct it?

....

Why is there a punctuation mistake in sentence 9? How would you correct the sentence?

DIRECTIONS
Use the passage on the previous page to answer the questions below. Circle the letter beside the correct answer. The hints can help you find the correct answers.

1. How would you correct sentence 2?

   A. Insert a comma between *art* and the quotation mark.

   B. Delete the quotation marks.

   C. Insert a semicolon after *believed.*

   D. It is correct as is.

   Hint Look for a quotation-related punctuation error.

2. How should sentence 3 be correctly written?

   A. She named her favorites; Egyptian art—the Impressionists—and modern sculpture.

   B. She named her favorites, Egyptian art, the Impressionists, and modern sculpture.

   C. She named her favorites: Egyptian art, the Impressionists, and modern sculpture.

   D. It is correct as is.

   Hint What punctuation mark is used to formally introduce lists?

3. How should sentence 5 be correctly written?

   A. Monets painting, looked so real, from a distance.

   B. Monet's painting looked so real from a distance.

   C. Monets-painting looked so real from a distance.

   D. It is correct as is.

   Hint The painting belongs to Monet. What punctuation mark shows ownership?

4. How would you correct sentence 8?

   A. Italicize *Monet and Me.*

   B. Insert a colon after *called.*

   C. Put quotation marks around *Monet and Me.*

   D. It is correct as is.

   Hint What type of punctuation is used for an article or essay?

5. On the lines below, rewrite the last paragraph of the passage so that all punctuation is correct.

Step 3

Read the following passage and then answer the questions below.

Letter to the Editor

Dear Editor,

(1) In last week's article Feeling Tired for No Reason, the writer explained a condition called anemia. (2) I was thrilled to read that letter? (3) I am a high school student who suffered from anemia for several months before I realized my problem. (4) I had all of the following problems extreme exhaustion, low appetite, and headaches. (5) When my doctor finally tested my blood, she discovered the anemia right away. (6) I began eating foods with more iron in them. (7) My doctor also prescribed supplements. (8) I followed all my doctors instructions in several weeks I felt better.

(9) I hope that all your readers will get tested if they think they might be anemic.

Sincerely,
Adella Contreras

Circle the letter of the best answer.

1. Which punctuation rule is not followed in sentence 1?

   A. using a comma after an introductory phrase

   B. using an end mark at the end of a sentence

   C. putting quotation marks around the title of an article

   D. using an apostrophe to show ownership

2. How should you correct the punctuation mistake in sentence 4?

   A. Insert a colon after *problems*.

   B. Delete the commas.

   C. Use a question mark for the end punctuation.

   D. Put a semicolon after *extreme*.

3. What is the correct way to write sentence 8?

   A. I followed all my doctors' instructions, in several weeks I felt better.

   B. I followed all my doctor's instructions; in several weeks I felt better.

   C. I followed all my doctors— instructions in several weeks I felt better.

   D. It is correct as is.

4. What is the BEST way to correct the error in sentence 2?

   A. Change the question mark to an exclamation point.

   B. Insert a comma after *thrilled*.

   C. Add apostrophe *s* to *letter.*

   D. It is correct as is.

DIRECTIONS
Read the passage. Use the Reading Guide for tips that can help you identify punctuation errors as you read. Then answer the questions on the next page.

excerpted and adapted from

The Bird Study Book

by Thomas Gilbert Pearson

(1) It was on the twentieth of January, a number of years ago, that the writer was first delighted by the sight of a bald eagles nest. (2) It was in an enormous pine tree growing in a swamp in central Florida? (3) Being ambitious to examine its contents I determined to climb to the great nest in the topmost fork of the tree, over 130 feet above the earth. (4) By means of climbing irons and a rope that passed around the tree and around my body, I slowly ascended, nailing cleats for support as I advanced. (5) After two hours of toil, the nest was reached, another twenty minutes were required to tear aside enough of the structure to permit climbing up one of the limbs on which it rested. (6) In doing this there were brought to view several layers of decayed twigs pine straw and fish bones. (7) The birds' had been using the nest for many years. (8) Season after season the huge structure had been enlarged by additions; now it was nearly five feet in thickness and about four feet across the top.

(9) At the date it was found; it contained two fledglings perhaps three weeks old. (10) Having been led to believe that eagles were ferocious birds when their nests were approached, it was with feelings of relief that I noticed the parents flying about at long riflerange. (11) The female, which was the larger of the pair, once or twice swept within twenty yards of my head. (12) But she quickly veered off and resumed her former action of beating back and forth over the tree-tops two hundred yards away.

Reading Guide

What is the punctuation error in sentence 1?

Where is an additional comma needed in sentence 3?

How would you correct sentence 5?

What is the punctuation error in sentence 7?

How would you correct sentence 9?

DIRECTIONS
Now read each question. Circle the letter of the best answer.

1. How would you correct the punctuation mistake in sentence 1?

    A. Insert quotation marks around *bald eagles*.

    B. Insert a dash after *January*.

    C. Change *eagles* to *eagle's*.

    D. It is correct as is.

    Hint   To whom does the nest belong? How is ownership punctuated?

2. What is the punctuation error in sentence 2?

    A. The sentence should end with a period.

    B. *Central Florida* should be hyphenated.

    C. A semicolon should be placed after *swamp.*

    D. It is correct as is.

    Hint   Ask yourself whether the author is trying to tell the reader something or ask the reader something.

3. How would you correct the two punctuation mistakes in sentence 6?

    A. Insert colon after *view.*

    B. Add commas after *twigs* and *straw.*

    C. Place an apostrophe after *bones.*

    D. It is correct as is.

    Hint   The author lists what he finds in the layers. How should the list be punctuated?

4. Why is a semicolon used in sentence 8?

    A. It joins two sentences that have no conjunction.

    B. It introduces a list formally.

    C. It follows an introductory phrase.

    D. It shows ownership.

    Hint   The semicolon is used correctly. What are the two parts of the sentence on either side of the semicolon?

5. How would you correct the punctuation mistake in sentence 10?

    A. Add apostrophe *s* to *female*.

    B. Insert semicolon after *approached.*

    C. Hyphenate *riflerange.*

    D. It is correct as is.

    Hint   Which correction helps to clarify a word for the reader?

DIRECTIONS

This passage is an excerpt from the novel *Little Men* by Louisa May Alcott. Read the passage. Then answer the questions on the page.

excerpted and adapted from

Little Men

by Louisa May Alcott

(1) "Please, sir, is this Plumfield!" asked a ragged boy of the man who opened the great gate.

(2) "Yes—who sent you?"

(3) "Mr. Laurence. I have got a letter for the lady" answered the boy.

(4) "Go up to the house and give it to her she'll see to you, little chap."

(5) The man spoke pleasantly, and the boy went on, feeling cheered. (6) Nat saw a large square house before him with an oldfashioned porch, wide steps, and lights shining in many windows. (7) Neither curtains nor shutters; hid the cheerful glimmer. (8) Pausing before he rang, Nat saw many little shadows dancing on the walls heard the pleasant hum of young voices and felt that it was hardly possible that the light and warmth and comfort within could be for a homeless "little chap" like him.

(9) "I hope the lady will see to me," he thought and gave a timid rap with the bronze knocker, which was a jolly griffins head.

(10) A rosy-faced maid opened the door. (11) She smiled as she took the letter which he silently offered. (12) She seemed used to receiving strange boys, for she pointed to a seat in the hall and asked him to wait there.

(13) Nat found plenty to amuse him while he waited; he stared about him curiously. (14) The house seemed swarming with boys. (15) Two large rooms on the right were evidently schoolrooms. (16) Desks, maps, blackboards, and books were scattered about. (17) An open fire burned on the hearth; several lads lay on their backs before it. (18) Quite undisturbed by the racket all about him, a tall youth was practicing on the flute in one corner. (19) Two or three others were jumping over the desks.

DIRECTIONS
Read each question. Circle the letter of the best answer.

1. How should you correct sentence 1?

   A. Change the exclamation point to a question mark.

   B. Delete the two commas.

   C. Insert a dash after *asked.*

   D. It is correct as is.

2. What rule is NOT followed in sentence 3?

   A. using commas between items in a list

   B. using a dash to emphasize a point

   C. using a colon to separate hours and minutes

   D. placing a comma inside the end of a quotation

3. What is the correct way to write sentence 4?

   A. "Go up to the house and give it to her—she'll see to you, little chap."

   B. "Go up to the house and give it to her; she'll see to you, little chap."

   C. "Go up to the house and give it to her, she'll see to you little chap."

   D. It is correct as is.

4. How can you correct sentence 6?

   A. Hyphenate *oldfashioned.*

   B. Delete the commas.

   C. Italicize *square house.*

   D. It is correct as is.

5. What rule explains why there is a comma after the word *rang* in sentence 8?

   A. Place a comma after items in a list.

   B. Use a comma to show the end of a sentence.

   C. Use a comma to separate two independent clauses with a conjunction.

   D. Place a comma after an introductory phrase.

6. How can you correct sentence 9?

   A. Delete the comma after *me.*

   B. Insert a semicolon after *thought.*

   C. Change *griffins* to *griffin's.*

   D. Hyphenate *bronze knocker.*

7. What is the correct way to write sentence 13?

   A. Nat found plenty to amuse him while he waited he stared about him curiously.

   B. Nat found plenty to amuse him while he waited, he stared about him curiously.

   C. Nat found plenty to amuse him, while he waited he stared about him curiously.

   D. It is correct as is.

8. On a separate sheet of paper, rewrite paragraph 5, fixing all punctuation. Explain why punctuation is important and identify three punctuation errors.

Lesson 3 • Capitalization

Step 1

Capitalization is the use of upper case or capital letters.

Always capitalize:

- The first word in any sentence or interjection.
  Ouch! You really hurt my finger.

- The first word of quotations that contain complete sentences.
  "Do not dwell in the past; do not dream of the future, but concentrate the mind on the present moment." —Buddha

- The pronoun *I*
  Did you realize I had won the spelling bee?

- Proper nouns, including people's names, geographical names, periods of time, months, days of the week, specific events, organizations, languages, holidays, nationalities, religions, deities, religious texts, and special objects
  When Sammy visited New York, he saw the Statue of Liberty.
  For Independence Day, we traveled to Philadelphia.

- Proper adjectives
  The American people voted last week.`
  The Labor Day celebration was the biggest the town had ever had.

These are some common capitalization errors:

Capitalization Error	Correct Capitalization
Emily dickinson once said, "to live is so startling it leaves little time for anything else."	Emily Dickinson once said, "To live is so startling it leaves little time for anything else."
the taj mahal is one of india's most famous sites.	The Taj Mahal is one of India's most famous sites.

DIRECTIONS
Read these sentences. **Think** **will help you answer each question.**

(1) In the 1920s, the astronomer Edwin hubble recognized galaxies outside our own.
(2) he believed that the universe is constantly expanding.

1. Which word should be capitalized in sentence 1?

   A. astronomer

   B. hubble

   C. recognized

   D. galaxies

2. Which word in sentence 2 should begin with a capital letter?

   A. he

   B. universe

   C. constantly

   D. expanding

Think

1. Reread the question. What is it about?

   Think It is a question about a word not being capitalized.

2. What must you do to answer the question?

   Think I must figure out which answer choice contains a word that should be capitalized. I must think about how certain words require capital letters.

3. Try out each answer choice.

   Think The words *astronomer* and *galaxies* are nouns, but they are not specific nouns, so they do not require capitalization. *Recognized* is a verb, and verbs are not capitalized unless they are at the beginning of a sentence. *Hubble* is part of someone's name, so it should be capitalized.

4. Choose the BEST answer.

   Think Answer B is the best answer.

Think

1. Reread the question. What is it about?

   Think It is a question about a missing capital letter.

2. What must you do to answer the question?

   Think I must remember the rules of capitalization.

3. Try out each answer choice.

   Think The word *universe* is not capitalized because it is not a proper noun. Neither *constantly* nor *expanding* requires capitalization. The word *he* is not usually capitalized, but it comes at the beginning of a sentence here.

4. Choose the BEST answer.

   Think Answer A is the best answer.

DIRECTIONS
Read this paragraph. Then circle the best answer to each question below. The hints can help you find the correct answers.

(1) Next sunday night is the Super Bowl. (2) I can't wait for the party because my friend sabir is going to watch american football for the first time. (3) He just moved here from Pakistan last June. (4) to him, football still means soccer!

1. How can you make sentence 1 correct?

   A.   Capitalize *sunday.*

   B.   Capitalize *night.*

   C.   Lowercase *Super Bowl.*

   D.   It is correct as is.

Hint	Is any word in the sentence a proper noun?

2. How should sentence 2 be written correctly?

   A.   I can't wait for the party because my friend sabir is going to watch american Football for the first time.

   B.   I can't wait for the party because my friend Sabir is going to watch American football for the first time.

   C.   I can't wait for the party because my Friend Sabir is going to watch american football for the first time.

   D.   It is correct as is.

Hint	Proper nouns and proper adjectives should always be capitalized.

3. How would you correct sentence 3?

   A.   Capitalize *moved.*

   B.   Capitalize *here.*

   C.   Capitalize *last.*

   D.   It is correct as is.

Hint	Does the sentence begin with a capital letter? Are all proper nouns and adjectives capitalized?

4. How should sentence 4 be written correctly?

   A.   to him, Football still means soccer!

   B.   to him, football still means Soccer!

   C.   To him, football still means soccer!

   D.   It is correct as is.

Hint	What capitalization rules should apply in this sentence? Are there proper nouns to consider?

5. Rewrite these sentences so that all capitalization is correct.

   the butter bakery now sells several varieties of cupcakes. When greta has her birthday on thursday, we are going to serve chocolate cupcakes.

   _____

   _____

   _____

One of the most important capitalization rules is to capitalize proper nouns and adjectives. **Proper nouns** and **adjectives** are very specific names. For example, the word *tower* is not capitalized when it stands alone, but the name *Eiffel Tower* is always capitalized.

Additionally, you should always capitalize:

- The first letter in abbreviated titles such as *Ms., Mr., Mrs., Jr., Sr.* and *Dr.*
  Dr. Marshall delivered babies at different hospitals all over town.

- A person's title when used in direct address
  Are you planning to attend the rally, Professor?

- Titles of government officials when followed by a proper name
  Mayor Canfield addressed the school children.

- The first word and key words in titles of books, periodicals, plays, movies, and other works of art
  My favorite movie is *Gone with the Wind.*

DIRECTIONS
Read the story. Use the Reading Guide for tips. Then answer the questions on the next page.

Lima, Peru

(1) The city of lima, peru, lies on the coast of the country. (2) From there, the city runs inland along the rímac river for 25 miles. (3) it is the largest city in the country, as well as the capital. (4) As many as one-third of all Peruvians live there.

(5) The city was founded in 1535 by francisco pizarro, who was part of the spanish force that invaded the area. (6) In 1746, most of Lima was destroyed by an earthquake. (7) Not until 1821 was Peru freed from Spanish control.

(8) lima is well-known for some of its famous churches and monasteries, such as the lima cathedral. (9) Many of these churches exhibit incan gold and andean silver in their decorations. (10) The city also houses the museum of the inquisition, which gives evidence of torture during times past.

Reading Guide

What is the mistake in sentence 2?

....

What capitalization rule is not followed in sentence 3? How would you correct it?

....

What capitalization rule is broken in sentence 7, if any?

DIRECTIONS
Use the passage on the previous page to answer the questions below. Circle the letter beside the correct answer. The hints can help you find the correct answers.

1.   How would you correct sentence 1?

   A.   Capitalize *city.*

   B.   Capitalize *lima* and *peru.*

   C.   Capitalize *coast* and *country.*

   D.   It is correct as is.

   > **Hint**   Look for geographical proper nouns in this sentence.

2.   How would you correctly rewrite sentence 5?

   A.   The city was founded in 1535 by francisco pizarro, who was part of the Spanish force that invaded the area.

   B.   The city was founded in 1535 by Francisco Pizarro, who was part of the spanish force that invaded the area.

   C.   The city was founded in 1535 by Francisco Pizarro, who was part of the Spanish force that invaded the area.

   D.   It is correct as is.

   > **Hint**   Capitalization rules apply both to proper nouns and proper adjectives.

3.   How would you correct sentence 9?

   A.   Capitalize *churches.*

   B.   Capitalize *gold* and *silver.*

   C.   Capitalize *incan* and *andean.*

   D.   It is correct as is.

   > **Hint**   What is the capitalization rule about proper adjectives?

4.   How would you correctly rewrite sentence 10?

   A.   The city also houses the Museum of the Inquisition, which gives evidence of torture during times past.

   B.   The City also houses the museum of the inquisition, which gives evidence of torture during times past.

   C.   The city also houses the museum of the inquisition, which gives evidence of torture during Times Past.

   D.   It is correct as is.

   > **Hint**   Names of specific places should have capital letters.

5.   On the lines below, rewrite the last paragraph of the passage so that all capitalization is correct.

   _____

   _____

   _____

   _____

DIRECTIONS
Read this sample student essay about the author J. S. Fletcher, and then answer the questions below.

J. S. Fletcher, Author

(1) Many people have never heard of the author J. S. Fletcher. (2) My neighbor ms. Florence introduced me to his writing last summer. (3) It changed my whole august because I began reading all fletcher's work.

(4) The first book i read was *the middle temple murder.* (5) Published in 1918, this book contains all the action and suspense you might expect from a good crime novel today. (6) But the language is more beautiful and interesting than most popular fiction I read.

(7) Fletcher was born in Halifax, England, in 1863. (8) Although he worked as a journalist and studied law, he is most famous for his crime novels.

(9) Even U.S. president Woodrow Wilson enjoyed Fletcher's novels. (10) If he read Fletcher's work, then I think it's worth a try, don't you?

Circle the letter of the best answer.

1. Which capitalization rule is not followed in sentence 2?

   A. Capitalize the first word of a sentence.

   B. Capitalize abbreviated titles.

   C. Capitalize key words in book titles.

   D. Capitalize the pronoun *I*.

2. How should you correct the capitalization mistake(s) in sentence 3?

   A. Capitalize *august.*

   B. Capitalize *fletcher's.*

   C. Capitalize *august* and *fletcher's.*

   D. It is correct as is.

3. What is the correct way to write sentence 4?

   A. The first book I read was *The Middle Temple Murder.*

   B. The first book I read was *the middle temple murder.*

   C. The first book i read was *the Middle Temple Murder.*

   D. It is correct as is.

4. Which capitalization rule is not followed in sentence 9?

   A. Capitalize a person's title in direct address.

   B. Capitalize religions and deities.

   C. Capitalize the first word in an interjection.

   D. Capitalize titles of government officials when followed by a proper noun.

DIRECTIONS
Read the story. Use the Reading Guide for tips that can help you identify capitalization errors as you read. Then answer the questions on the next page.

adapted and excerpted from

The Getting of Wisdom

by Henry Handel Richardson

(1) As long as the coach rolled down the main street, laura sat bolt upright at the window. (2) She heard people telling one another that this was little miss rambotham going to school. (3) She was particularly glad that just as they went past the Commercial Hotel, Miss Perrotet, the landlord's red-haired daughter, should put her fuzzy head out of the window. (4) Miss perrotet had also been to boarding school, and thought very highly of herself in consequence, though it had only been for a year. (5) At the National Bank the manager's wife waved a friendly hand to the children. (6) At the royal mail hotel where they drew up for passengers or commissions, Mrs. Paget, the stout landlady, came out, smoothing down her black satin apron.

(7) "Well, I'm sure i wonder your ma likes sendin' you off so alone."

(8) The ride had comforted Pin a little, but when they had passed the chief Stores and the flourmill, and came to a part of the road with fewer houses, Her tears broke out afresh. (9) the very last house was left behind and o'Donnell dismounted and opened the door. (10) He lifted the three out one by one, shaking his head in humorous dismay at pin, and as little frank showed signs of beginning, too, by puckering up his face, the kindly man tried to make them laugh by asking if he had the stomachache. (11) Laura had one more glimpse of the children standing hand in hand—even in her trouble Pin did not forget her charges—then a sharp bend in the road hid them from her sight.

Reading Guide

What word should be capitalized in sentence 1?
....

Why is *National Bank* capitalized in sentence 5?
....

What words should be capitalized in sentence 7?
....

Sentence 8 has too many capital letters. What are the two mistakes in this sentence?
....

Why are the words *Laura* and *Pin* capitalized in sentence 11?

DIRECTIONS
Now read each question. Circle the letter of the best answer.

1. How should sentence 2 be written correctly?

   A. She heard people telling one another that this was little Miss Rambotham going to school.

   B. She heard people telling one another that this was little miss Rambotham going to school.

   C. She heard People telling one another that this was little miss rambotham going to school.

   D. It is correct as is.

   Hint Both capitalization errors in this sentence are related to a person's title and name.

2. What word should be capitalized in sentence 4?

   A. perrotet

   B. boarding

   C. school

   D. It is correct as is.

   Hint Which word is a specific name, rather than a generic one?

3. How would you correct the capitalization mistakes in sentence 6?

   A. lowercase *Mrs. Paget*

   B. capitalize *royal*

   C. capitalize *royal mail hotel*

   D. It is correct as is.

   Hint Ask yourself about geographical places within the sentence. What mistakes do you see?

4. How should sentence 9 be written correctly?

   A. the very last house was left behind and O'Donnell dismounted and opened the door.

   B. The very last house was left behind and o'Donnell dismounted and opened the door.

   C. The very last house was left behind and O'Donnell dismounted and opened the door.

   D. It is correct as is.

   Hint You need to think of two different capitalization rules here.

5. What two words should be capitalized in sentence 10?

   A. *humorous* and *dismay*

   B. *pin* and *frank*

   C. *one* and *one*

   D. *puckering* and *frank*

   Hint Which two words represent specific people in the story?

DIRECTIONS
Read this excerpt from the introduction to *The Book of Art for Young People,* first published in 1909. Then answer the questions on the next page.

adapted and excerpted from

The Book of Art for Young People

by Agnes Conway and Sir Martin Conway

Introduction

(1) Almost the pleasantest thing in the world is to be told a splendid story by a really nice person. (2) There is not the least occasion for the story to be true; indeed i think that untrue stories are the best.

(3) But if I might choose the person to tell me the kind of story i like to listen to, it would be some one who could draw pictures for me while talking—pictures like those of tenniel in *alice in wonderland*. (4) How much better we know alice herself and all the rest of them from the pictures than even from the story itself. (5) But my story-teller should not only draw the pictures while he talked, but he should paint them too. (6) I want to see the sky blue and the grass green, and I want red cloaks and blue bonnets and pink cheeks and all the bright colors, and some gold and silver too.

(7) now, the old pictures you see in the picture galleries are just like that, only the people that painted them didn't invent the stories but merely illustrated stories.

(8) There is a delightful old picture painted on a wall away off at assisi, in italy. (9) It shows st. francis preaching to a lot of birds, and the birds are all listening to him and looking pleased. (10) Now, St. Francis was a real man and such a dear person too, but i don't suppose half the stories told about him were really true. (11) Yet we can pretend they were and that's just what the painter helps us to do.

(12) don't you know all the games that begin with "let's pretend"? (13) Well, that's art. (14) Art is pretending, or most of it is.

DIRECTIONS
Now read each question. Circle the letter of the best answer.

1. How should you correct sentence 2?

    A. Capitalize *story*.

    B. Capitalize *indeed*.

    C. Capitalize *I*.

    D. It is correct as is.

2. How should sentence 3 be written correctly?

    A. But if I might choose the person to tell me the kind of story i like to listen to, it would be some one who could draw pictures for me while talking—pictures like those of tenniel in *Alice in wonderland*.

    B. But if I might choose the person to tell me the kind of story I like to listen to, it would be some one who could draw pictures for me while talking—pictures like those of Tenniel in *Alice in Wonderland*.

    C. But if I might choose the person to tell me the kind of story I like to listen to, it would be some one who could draw pictures for me while talking—pictures like those of Tenniel in *alice in wonderland*.

    D. It is correct as is.

3. What rule should be used correctly in sentence 4?

    A. Capitalize the first letter of abbreviated titles.

    B. Capitalize proper nouns.

    C. Capitalize works of art.

    D. The sentence is correct.

4. How should you correct sentence 5?

    A. Capitalize *story-teller*.

    B. Capitalize *pictures*.

    C. Capitalize *paint*.

    D. It is correct as is.

5. What word should be capitalized in sentence 7?

    A. now

    B. pictures

    C. galleries

    D. It is correct as is.

6. What rule is not followed in sentence 8?

    A. Capitalize proper adjectives.

    B. Capitalize the first word in a quotation.

    C. Capitalize periods of time.

    D. Capitalize geographical names.

7. How should sentence 12 be written correctly?

    A. Don't you know all the games that begin with "let's pretend"?

    B. don't you know all the games that begin with "Let's pretend"?

    C. Don't you know all the games that begin with "Let's pretend"?

    D. It is correct as is.

8. On a separate sheet of paper, rewrite paragraph 4. Fix all capitalization errors.

Lesson 4 • Subject-Verb Agreement

Step 1

A **subject** is a noun in a sentence that performs the action. **Subject-verb agreement** is the relationship between a sentence's subject and its verb.

Here are some key rules for subject-verb agreement:

- A single subject must have a singular verb and a plural subject must have a plural verb.
  Singular: <u>Isaac believes</u> the football team will do well this year.
  Plural: <u>We are planting</u> seeds in the backyard.

- Compound subjects (more than one subject) joined by *and* are treated as plural and use a plural verb.
  <u>A bluebird and a crow</u> appear in the window.

- Two singular subjects joined by the conjunctions *or* or *nor* use a singular verb.
  A good <u>grade</u> or <u>score</u> causes me to smile.

- When a single subject is joined to a plural subject with *or* or *nor*, the subject nearest to the verb decides agreement.
  Neither my <u>friends</u> nor <u>Albert</u> is feeling well.
  Neither <u>Albert</u> nor my <u>friends are</u> feeling well.

- When a subject comes after the verb, the two must still agree.
  Below the bridge <u>live</u> two <u>kittens</u>.

- Collective nouns act as a single unit even if they consist of multiple members. Some examples include: *audience, class, club, family*, and *committee*. Collective nouns use singular verbs.
  Our <u>class reports</u> to the other class weekly.

Here are some common subject-verb agreement errors.

Subject-Verb Agreement Error	Correct Subject-Verb Agreement
The boys tosses the ball to the coach.	The boys toss the ball to the coach.
A bun and a pickle makes a sandwich perfect.	A bun and a pickle make a sandwich perfect.
The soccer club meet each Tuesday.	The soccer club meets each Tuesday.

DIRECTIONS
Read these sentences. Think will help you answer each question.

(1) Henrietta march into her sister's room with a frown on her face. (2) "I thought this family were a team," she shouts.

1. Which word causes the subject-verb agreement error in sentence 1?

  A. march

  B. sister's

  C. room

  D. frown

2. Which word BEST replaces *were* in sentence 2?

  A. are

  B. will be

  C. was

  D. is

Think

1. Reread the question. What is it about?

  Think   It is a question about a subject-verb agreement error.

2. What must you do to answer the question?

  Think   I must figure out which answer choice contains the word that creates the error.

3. Try out each answer choice.

  Think   The words *sister's, room,* and *frown* are not the subject or the verb in the sentence, so they do not create the error. The subject is *Henrietta*, so the verb must be singular to agree with the subject. In sentence 1, *march* creates the error.

4. Choose the BEST answer.

  Think   Answer A is the best answer.

Think

1. Reread the question. What is it about?

  Think   It is a question about replacing an incorrect word in the sentence.

2. What must you do to answer the question?

  Think   I must remember the rules of subject-verb agreement.

3. Try out each answer choice.

  Think   The word *are* still has a subject-verb agreement problem. The words *will be* do not make sense in this sentence. The word *family* is singular, so it requires a singular verb.

4. Choose the BEST answer.

  Think   Answer C is the best answer.

DIRECTIONS
Read this paragraph. Then circle the best answer to each question below. The hints can help you find the correct answers.

(1) Under my bed are a box of letters from my grandmother. (2) My grandmother live in Indonesia right now because she works as a diplomat. (3) My brother and I has not seen her for over a year. (4) But our family is traveling there during spring break to visit.

1. How can you make sentence 1 correct?

   A. Change *bed* to *beds.*

   B. Change *letters* to *letter.*

   C. Change *are* to *is.*

   D. It is correct as is.

   Hint   What are the subject and verb?

2. How should sentence 2 be written correctly?

   A. My grandmother lives in Indonesia right now because she works as a diplomat.

   B. My grandmother live in Indonesia right now because she work as a diplomat.

   C. My grandmother lived in Indonesia right now because she works as a diplomat.

   D. It is correct as is.

   Hint   Is the subject singular or plural?

3. How would you correct sentence 3?

   A. Change *brother* to *brothers.*

   B. Change *has* to *have.*

   C. Change *has* to *will.*

   D. It is correct as is.

   Hint   The subject is a compound subject.

4. How should sentence 4 be written correctly?

   A. But our family are traveling there during spring break to visit.

   B. But our family be traveling there during spring break to visit.

   C. But our family were traveling there during spring break to visit.

   D. It is correct as is.

   Hint   What is the rule for using a collective noun that acts as a single unit?

5. Rewrite these sentences so that all subject-verb agreement is correct.

   (1) Frederick study the weather because he is becoming a meteorologist. (2) Hurricanes and tornadoes is currently his main interests.

   _____

   _____

   _____

Step 2

In any sentence, the verb must agree with the subject. A subject can either be **singular** (one person or thing) or **plural** (more than one person or thing).

Here are some additional subject-verb agreement rules:

- Singular indefinite pronouns require singular verbs: *anybody, anyone, anything, each, either, every, everybody, everyone, everything, neither, nobody, no one, nothing, somebody, someone, something.*

  <u>Everyone feels</u> excited about the concert.

- Plural indefinite pronouns require plural verbs: *both, few, many, others, several*

  <u>Several</u> of the students <u>feel</u> excited about the concert.

- The following pronouns can be singular or plural depending on whether the antecedent is singular or plural: *all, any, more, most, none, some.*

  <u>Most</u> of the <u>ducks</u> <u>swim</u> around the pond.

  <u>Most</u> of the <u>cake</u> <u>is</u> gone.

DIRECTIONS
Read the story. Use the Reading Guide for tips. Then answer the questions on the next page.

Mangroves

(1) In tropical coastal areas, several types of trees grows along the silty coastline. (2) The various trees that grow in the still, swampy waters is called mangroves. (3) Unlike other trees, mangroves is not harmed by the salt water that comes in and out with the tide. (4) The roots of the trees grows right in the shallow water, providing a harbor for certain creatures. (5) Snapping turtles and fiddler crabs feed there. (6) Other animals do not see them because of the dark water and floating plants. (7) The feet of snapping turtles is designed to move on land and under water.

(8) The leaves of the mangrove provides a place for iguanas and snakes to lie in the sun. (9) Other leafy plants grows in the waters, as well. (10) A water lettuce, for example, float above the water, with its roots dangling below the surface.

Reading Guide

What is the mistake in sentence 2?

....

What subject-verb agreement rule is not followed in sentence 4? How would you correct it?

....

What rule is broken in sentence 10?

DIRECTIONS
Use the passage on the previous page to answer the questions below. Circle the letter beside the correct answer. The hints can help you find the correct answers.

1. How would you correct sentence 1?

   A. Change *areas* to *area*.

   B. Change *grows* to *grow*.

   C. Change *grows* to *growed*.

   D. It is correct as is.

   Hint The subject of this sentence is *types*.

2. How should sentence 3 be correctly written?

   A. Unlike other trees, mangroves is not harmed by the salt water that come in and out with the tide.

   B. Unlike other tree, mangroves is not harmed by the salt water that comes in and out with the tide.

   C. Unlike other trees, mangroves are not harmed by the salt water that comes in and out with the tide.

   D. It is correct as is.

   Hint What type of verb does a plural subject take?

3. How should sentence 5 be correctly written?

   A. Snapping turtles and fiddler crabs feeds there.

   B. Snapping turtle and fiddler crab feed there.

   C. Snapping turtles and fiddler crabs fed there.

   D. It is correct as is.

   Hint What is the rule about compound subjects joined by *and*?

4. How would you correct sentence 7?

   A. Change *is* to *are*.

   B. Change *feet* to *feets*.

   C. Change *move* to *moves*.

   D. It is correct as is.

   Hint What is the subject of the sentence? Is it singular or plural?

5. On the lines below, rewrite the last paragraph of the passage so that all subject-verb agreement is correct.

   _____

   _____

   _____

   _____

   _____

   _____

Step 3

DIRECTIONS
Read this sample student essay about video games, and then answer the questions below.

Being Different, But Okay

(1) Every day at school, students converses about new video consoles, systems, and games. (2) In the past, this has made me feel like an outsider because I do not own a video game system. (3) Most of my friends has several systems of some kind or other.

(4) Don't get me wrong—I enjoy video games a great deal and have played them at friends' houses. (5) But my parents think I should use my spare time playing sports, reading good books, and exploring the world away from a screen. (6) These rules have frustrated me in the past, as you might imagine. (7) How are a teenager supposed to avoid video games?

(8) But this year I think I have begun to change. (9) My parents may have the right idea after all. (10) Together we have spent more time hiking, reading, and playing tennis. (11) I want to trust my parents' judgment. (12) Even some of my friends is vowing to start spending more time outdoors, as well!

Circle the letter of the best answer.

1. Which subject-verb agreement rule is not followed in sentence 1?

   A. Two subjects joined by *and* are treated as a plural subject.

   B. When a subject comes after the verb, the two must still agree.

   C. Collective nouns act as a single unit.

   D. Plural subjects take plural verbs.

2. How should sentence 3 be corrected?

   A. Change *has* to *have*.

   B. Change *has* to *had*.

   C. Change *friends* to *friend*.

   D. It is correct as is.

3. What is the correct way to write sentence 7?

   A. How are a teenagers supposed to avoid video games?

   B. How is a teenager supposed to avoid video games?

   C. How are a teenager supposed to avoids video games?

   D. It is correct as is.

4. How should sentence 12 be corrected?

   A. Change *friends* to *friend*.

   B. Change *is* to *will be*.

   C. Change *is* to *are*.

   D. It is correct as is.

DIRECTIONS
Read the passage. Use the Reading Guide for tips that can help you identify subject-verb agreement errors as you read. Then answer the questions on the next page.

adapted and excerpted from

Beautiful Stories from Shakespeare

by E. Nesbit

(1) In the register of baptisms of the parish church of Stratford-upon-Avon in Warwickshire, England, appear the entry of the baptism of William, the son of John Shakspeare. (2) Under the date of April 26, 1564, it are listed. (3) The entry is in Latin: "Gulielmus filius Johannis Shakspeare."

(4) The date of William Shakespeare's birth have usually been taken as three days before this baptism.

(5) Shakespeare's father, while an alderman at Stratford, appear to have been unable to write his name. (6) But as at that time nine men out of ten was content to make their mark for a signature, the fact is not specially to his discredit.

(7) The traditions and other sources of information about the occupation of Shakespeare's father differs. (8) He is described as a butcher, a woolstapler, and a glover. (9) He was a landed proprietor and cultivator of his own land even before his marriage to Mary Arden. (10) William were the third child. (11) The two older than he were daughters, and both probably died in infancy. (12) After him was born three sons and a daughter.

(13) In 1568 Shakespeare's father was the high bailiff or chief magistrate of Stratford. (14) For many years afterwards he held the position of alderman as he had done for three years before. (15) As a result, it is natural to suppose that William Shakespeare would get the best education that Stratford could afford. (16) The free school of the town was open to all boys. (17) Like all the grammar schools of that time, this one was under the direction of men who were qualified to diffuse that sound scholarship which was once the boast of England. (18) His father could not have procured for him a better education anywhere. (19) Shakespeare's works abounds with evidences that he must have been solidly grounded in the learning, properly so called, taught in the grammar schools.

Reading Guide

What word is used incorrectly in sentence 1?

....

How would you correct sentence 2?

....

In sentence 5, what subject-verb agreement rule is broken?

....

How would you rewrite sentence 7 to correct the subject-verb agreement error?

....

What word is used incorrectly in sentence 12?

DIRECTIONS
Now read each question. Circle the letter of the best answer.

1. How would you correct the subject-verb agreement error in sentence 1?

   A. Change *register* to *registers.*

   B. Change *appear* to *appears.*

   C. Change *entry* to *entries.*

   D. It is correct as is.

   Hint In this sentence the subject appears after the verb.

2. What subject-verb agreement rule is broken in sentence 4?

   A. Single subjects take singular verbs.

   B. Compound subjects take plural verbs.

   C. Collective nouns take singular verbs.

   D. When a subject comes after the verb, the two must still agree.

   Hint What is the subject of this sentence? Is it singular or plural?

3. Which word creates the subject-verb agreement error in sentence 6?

   A. was

   B. content

   C. make

   D. specially

   Hint Although this sentence has a lot of words, you need to identify the subject before you can determine the error.

4. How would you rewrite sentence 10 to correct the subject-verb agreement error?

   A. William are the third child.

   B. Williams were the third child.

   C. William was the third child.

   D. It is correct as is.

   Hint Because *William* refers to only one person, the verb must be singular.

5. How would you correct the subject-verb agreement error in sentence 19?

   A. Change *Shakespeare's* to *Shakespeare.*

   B. Change *abounds* to *abound.*

   C. Change *have* to *has.*

   D. It is correct as is.

   Hint In your mind, delete everything but the subject and the verb. The subject is *works.* What rule applies to a plural subject?

DIRECTIONS
Read this passage. Then answer the questions on the next page.

adapted and excerpted from

The Book of Tea

by Kakuzo Okakura

(1) Tea began as a medicine and grew into a beverage. (2) In China, in the eighth century, it entered the realm of poetry as one of the polite amusements. (3) The fifteenth century saw Japan ennoble it into a religion of aestheticism called "Teaism." (4) Teaism are founded on the adoration of the beautiful among the sordid facts of everyday existence.

(5) The long isolation of Japan from the rest of the world have been highly favorable to the development of Teaism. (6) Our home and habits, costume and cuisine, porcelain, lacquer, painting—our very literature—all has been subject to its influence. (7) No student of Japanese culture could ever ignore its presence. (8) It has permeated the elegance of the noble and the abode of the humble. (9) Our peasants have learned to arrange flowers, our meanest laborer to offer his salutation to the rocks and waters. (10) In our common way of speaking, we speaks of the man "with no tea" in him. (11) And we criticizes the untamed person who runs riot in the springtide of emancipated emotions as one "with too much tea" in him.

(12) The outsider may indeed wonder at this seeming much ado about nothing. (13) What a tempest in a tea cup, he will say. (14) But when we consider how small after all the cup of human enjoyment is, how soon overflowed with tears, how easily drained to the dregs in our quenchless thirst for infinity, we shall not blame ourselves for making so much of the tea cup.

(15) Mankind have done worse. (16) In the worship of Bacchus, we have sacrificed too freely. (17) We have even transfigured the gory image of Mars. (18) Why not consecrates ourselves to the queen of the Camelias, and revel in the warm stream of sympathy that flows from her altar? (19) In the liquid amber within the ivory porcelain, the initiated may touches the sweet reticence of Confucius, the piquancy of Laotse, and the ethereal aroma of Sakyamuni himself.

DIRECTIONS
Now read each question. Circle the letter of the best answer.

1. What is the correct way to write sentence 4?

   A. Teaism will be founded on the adoration of the beautiful among the sordid facts of everyday existence.

   B. Teaism were founded on the adoration of the beautiful among the sordid facts of everyday existence.

   C. Teaism is founded on the adoration of the beautiful among the sordid facts of everyday existence.

   D. It is correct as is.

2. What correction should be made to sentence 5 so that there is subject-verb agreement?

   A. Change *isolation* to *isolations.*

   B. Change *rest* to *rests.*

   C. Change *have* to *has.*

   D. It is correct as is.

3. How should sentence 7 be changed to correct for subject-verb agreement?

   A. Change *student* to *students.*

   B. Change *ignore* to *ignores.*

   C. Change *presence* to *presences.*

   D. It is correct as is.

4. What is the correct way to write sentence 10?

   A. In our common way of speaking, we speak of the man "with no tea" in him.

   B. In our common way of speaking, we speaked of the man "with no tea" in him.

   C. In our common way of speaking, they speaks of the man "with no tea" in him.

   D. It is correct as is.

5. How can you correct sentence 11?

   A. Change *criticizes* to *criticize.*

   B. Change *runs* to *run.*

   C. Change *emotions* to *emotion.*

   D. It is correct as is.

6. What rule should be used correctly in sentence 15?

   A. Compound subjects require plural verbs.

   B. Plural indefinite pronouns require plural verbs.

   C. When a subject comes after the verb, the two must still agree.

   D. Collective nouns use singular verbs.

7. On a separate sheet of paper, rewrite the final paragraph fixing all errors.

Lesson 5 • Parts of Speech

The four main **parts of speech** are nouns, verbs, adjectives, and adverbs.

Here is more information about the parts of speech:

- A **noun** names a person, place, thing, or idea.
  swimmer, downtown, clock, love

- **Proper nouns** are specific nouns which require capitalization.
  Philadelphia is a beautiful city.

- Most plural nouns are created by adding –*s* or –*es* to the singular form of the noun.
  violets; tomatoes

- In words ending in a *y* after a vowel, the plural is formed by adding –*s*. In words ending in a *y* after a consonant, the *y* is changed to *i* and –*es* is added.
  play—plays   berry—berries

- A **verb** shows action or state of being.
  The mystery novel <u>sells</u> well.
  Monica <u>feels</u> sick.

- Use proper verb tense to show when an action takes place.
  Present: Juan *walks* to school.
  Past: Juan *walked* to school yesterday.
  Future: Juan *will walk* to school tomorrow.

- An **adjective** describes a noun or pronoun.
  The <u>mystery</u> novel sells well.

- An **adverb** describes a verb, adjective, or adverb. It tells *how, when,* or *where*.
  The mystery novel sells <u>well</u>.
  The new tabby kitten was <u>nowhere</u>!
  <u>Frequently</u> the weather report is wrong.

These are some common errors in the use of parts of speech:

Error	Correction
Yesterday, the bunch of daisys sits on the mantel.	Yesterday, the bunch of daisies sat on the mantel.
We attended the performance next tuesday.	We will attend the performance next Tuesday.

DIRECTIONS
Read these sentences. Think will help you answer each question.

(1) When Mark returned to his old house in St. Louis, he was stunned. (2) The new owners had repainted the entire front of the house.

1. In sentence 1, what part of speech is the word *Mark*?

   A. noun

   B. verb

   C. adjective

   D. adverb

2. In sentence 2, the words *had repainted* are what part of speech?

   A. noun

   B. verb

   C adjective

   D adverb

Think

1. **Reread the question. What is it about?**

   Think It is a question about identifying a part of speech.

2. **What must you do to answer the question?**

   Think I must figure out which answer choice describes the word *Mark*. I must think about the definitions of each part of speech.

3. **Try out each answer choice.**

   Think The word *Mark* does not refer to an action (a verb). It does not describe a noun, a verb, or an adjective. Instead, the word is a person.

4. **Choose the BEST answer.**

   Think Answer A is the best answer.

Think

1. **Reread the question. What is it about?**

   Think It is a question about a part of speech.

2. **What must you do to answer the question?**

   Think I must remember what each part of speech is.

3. **Try out each answer choice.**

   Think The word *repainted* is not a person, place, thing, or idea (noun). It is not a descriptive word (adjective or adverb). Instead, the word tells what action happened.

4. **Choose the BEST answer.**

   Think Answer B is the best answer.

DIRECTIONS
Read this paragraph. Then circle the best answer to each question below.

(1) The brilliant stars shine on the field mice. (2) Hurriedly, they gather bits of grain from the ground. (3) Tomorrow, the farmer plowed the field, so the grain must be gathered today. (4) The mice take their grain to their various mice citys.

1. What part of speech is the word *brilliant* in sentence 1?

   A. noun

   B. verb

   C. adjective

   D. adverb

   Hint The word modifies *stars*. What part of speech describes nouns?

2. In sentence 2, what part of speech is the word *hurriedly*?

   A. noun

   B. verb

   C. adjective

   D. adverb

   Hint The word describes *how* the mice move.

3. How would you correct sentence 3?

   A. Tomorrow, the farmer did plow the field, so the grain must be gathered today.

   B. Tomorrow, the farmer plowed the field, so the grain will be gathered today.

   C. Tomorrow, the farmer will plow the field, so the grain must be gathered today.

   D. It is correct as is.

   Hint Which verb does not make sense given the time frame?

4. How should sentence 4 be written correctly?

   A. The mice take their grain to their various mice cities.

   B. The mice take their grain to their various mice cityies.

   C. The mice take their grain to their various mice city.

   D. It is correct as is.

   Hint What are the rules for making nouns plural?

5. Rewrite these sentences so that all parts of speech are used correctly.

We received many book in this year's book drive. My aunt donate a series of fantasys.

_____

_____

Adjectives and adverbs help to make nouns and verbs more specific. Here are some additional rules to remember about adjectives and adverbs:

- Capitalize proper adjectives
  <u>Diane's</u> necklace

- When comparing two nouns, use **comparative adjectives** by adding *–er* or using *more*.
  This cheese is *sweeter* than the cheddar from last week.
  You are *more* stubborn than your brother Joshua.

- When comparing more than two nouns, use **superlative adjectives** by adding *–est* or using *most*.
  This cheese is the *sweetest* of all the cheeses in the shop.
  You are the *most* stubborn member of this family.

- When comparing two verbs, use **comparative adverbs** by adding *–er* or by using *more*.
  Truman acts *happier* than Stanley.
  My Auntie Anne visits us *more* often than my Uncle Pete.

- When comparing more than two verbs, use **superlative adverbs** by adding *–est* or by using *most*.
  Truman acts the *happiest* of all my neighbors.
  Of all our relatives, my granddad visits us the *most*.

- Do not confuse adjectives and adverbs. Only adverbs can describe verbs.
  Incorrect: Maggie performed *good* last week at the concert.
  Correct: Maggie performed *well* last week at the concert.

DIRECTIONS
Read the story. Use the Reading Guide for tips.

A Weekend Dream

(1) After school on Friday, I was lying on my sister francie's bed.
(2) Earlier in the afternoon, I had finish my science exam.
(3) Although I had done pretty good, it had been a lot hardest than my last test.
(4) Now I will be thinking about what to do for the evening.
(5) I considered a movie or dinner at a restaurant. (6) Instant, I realized what I wanted. (7) Our family had worked all week long in our various activitys. (8) Mom wrote a report for work, and Dad had been digging up the garden in the backyard. (9) I knew Francie was exhausted from her babysitting job.
(10) For once, I wanted us to all be home together for a Friday night. (11) I marched quick into the living room and made my announcement. (12) "If all of you could stay home tonight, you would make me the happier girl in the world!"

Reading Guide

What is the mistake in sentence 1?

....

What part of speech rule is not followed in sentence 4? How would you correct it?

....

How should sentence 6 be corrected?

DIRECTIONS
Use the passage on the previous page to answer the questions below. Circle the letter beside the correct answer. The hints can help you find the correct answers.

1. How would you correct sentence 2?

   A. Change *Earlier* to *Earliest*.

   B. Change *had* to *have*.

   C. Change *finish* to *finished*.

   D. It is correct as is.

   Hint Read the sentence aloud and listen for the time error.

2. How should sentence 3 be correctly written?

   A. Although I had done pretty well, it had been a lot hardest than my last test.

   B. Although I had done pretty well, it had been a lot harder than my last test.

   C. Although I had done pretty good, it had been a lot harder than my last test.

   D. It is correct as is.

   Hint This sentence includes both an adverb and an adjective error.

3. How should sentence 7 be corrected?

   A. Change *had worked* to *will work*.

   B. Change *various* to *variously*.

   C. Change *activity* to *activities*.

   D. It is correct as is.

   Hint What is the rule about making nouns that end in *y* plural?

4. How should sentence 9 be written correctly?

   A. I knew Francie was exhausted from her babysit job.

   B. I knew Francie was exhausted from their babysitting job.

   C. I knew Francie will be exhausted from her babysitting job.

   D. It is correct as is.

   Hint Be sure that the nouns, verbs, adjectives, and adverbs are used correctly.

5. On the lines below, rewrite the last paragraph of the passage so that all parts of speech are used correctly.

_____

_____

_____

_____

_____

Step 3

Read the passage, and then answer the questions below.

Pastry Shops

(1) I admit it was a strange experiment. (2) But when I suggested researching pastry shops for a school project, my teacher approved enthusiastic.

(3) "It will make the project interesting for you," she said. (4) "It is also useful information! (5) I want to know the tastier shop in town."

(6) Here is the way my experiment worked. (7) Each day for a week, my dad and I visited several shops. (8) At each shop, we sampled bites of two or three pastrys. (9) In my notebook, we rated our samples with a number system. (10) Actually, my dad and I ended up disagreeing a lot. (11) He always thought the cheese danishes were sweeter than I did.

(12) On the day I presented my research findings at school, I brought the whole class a box of samples.

Circle the letter of the best answer.

1. What change should be made to sentence 2?

    A. Change *researching* to *research.*

    B. Change *shops* to *shoppes.*

    C. Change *enthusiastic* to *enthusiastically.*

    D. It is correct as is.

2. What is the correct way to write sentence 5?

    A. I want to know the tastiest shop in town.

    B. I want to know the more tasty shop in town.

    C. I want to know the most tastier shop in town.

    D. It is correct as is.

3. How should sentence 8 be corrected?

    A. Change *shops* to *Shops.*

    B. Change *pastrys* to *pastries.*

    C. Change *sampled* to *will sample.*

    D. It is correct as is.

4. In sentence 9, *number* is acting as which part of speech?

    A. noun

    B. verb

    C. adjective

    D. adverb

DIRECTIONS
Read the story. Use the Reading Guide for tips that can help you identify parts of speech errors as you read. Then answer the questions on the next page.

adapted and excerpted from

A Child's History of England

by Charles Dickens

(1) If you look at a map of the world, you will see, in the upper left-hand corner of the eastern hemisphere, two islandes lying in the sea. (2) They are England and Scotland, and Ireland. (3) England and Scotland form the greatest part of the two main islands. (4) Ireland is the next in size. (5) The little neighboring islands are chiefly little bits of Scotland.

(6) In the old days, a long, long while ago, these islands are in the same place, and the stormy sea roared round them, just as it roars now. (7) But the sea was not alive, then, with great ships and brave sailors, sailing to and from all parts of the world. (8) It was very lonely. (9) The islands lay solitary, in the great expanse of water. (10) The foaming waves dash against their cliffs, and the bleak winds blew over their forests. (11) But the winds and waves brought no adventurers to land upon the islands. (12) The islanders knew nothing of the rest of the world, and the rest of the world knew nothing of them.

(13) It is supposed that the Phoenicians, who were an ancient people, famous for carrying on trade, came in ships to these islands, and found that they produced tin and lead. (14) Both are very useful things and both produced to this very hour upon the sea-coast. (15) The most celebrated tin mines in Cornwall are, still, closely to the sea. (16) One of them, which I have seen, is so close to it that it is hollowed out underneath the ocean. (17) The miners say that in stormy weather, when they are at work down in that deep place, they can hear the noise of the waves thundering above their heads. (18) So, the phoenicians, coasting about the islands, would come, without much difficulty, to where the tin and lead were.

Reading Guide

What is the mistake in sentence 1?

....

What part of speech is the word *then* in sentence 7?

....

Identify the noun, verb, adverb, and adjective in sentence 8.

....

How would you make *sea-coast* in sentence 14 plural?

....

What is the error in sentence 18?

84

DIRECTIONS
Now read each question. Circle the letter of the best answer.

1. How should sentence 3 be written correctly?

   A. England and Scotland form the greater part of the two main islands.

   B. England and Scotland form the most great part of the two main islands.

   C. England and Scotland form the more great part of the two main islands.

   D. It is correct as is.

   Hint How should the comparative adjective form of *great* be written?

2. What part of speech is the word *chiefly* in sentence 5?

   A. noun

   B. verb

   C. adjective

   D. adverb

   Hint What does the word *chiefly* modify?

3. How would you correct the mistake in sentence 6?

   A. Change *roared* to *roars*.

   B. Change *are* to *were*.

   C. Change *stormy* to *Stormy*.

   D. It is correct as is.

   Hint Use proper verb tenses to show when actions take place.

4. What rule is broken in sentence 10?

   A. use of comparative adverbs

   B. use of proper verb tenses

   C. capitalization of proper adjectives

   D. formation of plural nouns

   Hint Look at both verbs in the sentence to see when this sentence occurs.

5. What change should be made to sentence 15?

   A. Change *celebrated* to *celebrate*.

   B. Change *still* to *stilly*.

   C. Change *closely* to *close*.

   D. It is correct as is.

   Hint An adverb needs to be changed to an adjective.

DIRECTIONS

Read this excerpt from Dorothy L. Sayers' novel *Whose Body?* Then answer the questions on the next page.

adapted and excerpted from

Whose Body?

by Dorothy L. Sayers

(1) Mr. Alfred Thipps was a small, nervous man, whose flaxen hair was beginning to abandon the unequal struggle with destiny. (2) Almost in the same breath with his first greeting, he made a self-conscious apology for it, murmuring something about having run against the dining-room door in the dark. (3) He was touched almost to tears by Lord Peter's thoughtfulness and condescension in calling.

(4) "I'm sure it's most kind of your lordship," he repeated, rapid blinking his weak little eyelids. (5) "I appreciate it very deeply, very deeply, indeed, and so would Mother, only she's so deaf. (6) I don't like to trouble you with making her understand. (7) It's been very hard all day," he added, "with the policemen in the house and all this commotion. (8) It's what Mother and me have never been used to, always living very retired, and it's most distressing to a man of regular habits. (9) I'm almost thankful Mother doesn't understand, for I'm sure it would worry her terrible if she was to know about it. (10) She was upset at first, but she's made up some idea of her own about it now. (11) I'm sure it's all for the best."

(12) The old lady who sits knitting by the fire nodded grim in response to a look from her son.

(13) The flat was the top one of the building and situated about the middle of the block. (14) Beyond were the back gardens of a parallel line of houses. (15) On the right rise the extensive edifice of St. Luke's Hospital with its grounds. (16) It was connected by a covered way to the residence of the famous surgeon, Sir Julian Freke, who directed the surgically side of the great new hospital. (17) In addition, he was known in harley Street as a distinguished neurologist with a highly individually point of view.

DIRECTIONS
Now read each question. Circle the letter of the best answer.

1. What part of speech is the word *unequal* in sentence 1?

    A. noun

    B. verb

    C. adjective

    D. adverb

2. How would you make the word *apology* in sentence 2 plural?

    A. apologys

    B. apologies

    C. apologyies

    D. apologieys

3. How can you correct sentence 4?

    A. Change *rapid* to *rapidly.*

    B. Change *repeated* to *repeats.*

    C. Change *weak* to *weakest.*

    D. It is correct as is.

4. What two words are both adverbs in sentence 5?

    A. *appreciate* and *it*

    B. *very* and *deeply*

    C. *indeed* and *Mother*

    D. *she's* and *deaf*

5. What is the error made in sentence 9?

    A. improper use of comparative adverbs

    B. improper use of proper verb tenses

    C. confusion of adjective and adverb

    D. improper formation of plural nouns

6. What is the BEST way to rewrite sentence 12?

    A. The old lady who sat knitting by the fire nodded grimly in response to a look from her son.

    B. The old lady who is sitting knitting by the fire nodded grim in responses to a look from her son.

    C. The old lady who sits knitting by the fire nods grim in response to a look from her son.

    D. It is correct as is.

7. What part of speech is the word *surgeon* in sentence 16?

    A. noun

    B. verb

    C. adjective

    D. adverb

8. On a separate sheet of paper, rewrite paragraph 4, correcting all errors.

Lesson 6 • Complete Sentences

Step 1

A **sentence** is a complete thought that contains a subject and a predicate. The **subject** is a noun or pronoun that tells who or what the sentence is about. This may be a single word or may include several words that describe the subject. The **predicate** contains a verb that tells something about the subject. This may be a single verb or may include several other words that modify the verb.

Here are some key rules for writing complete sentences:

- A **clause** is a group of words with a subject and a verb. An **independent clause** is a clause that stands alone.
  Brian teaches German.

- A **dependent** or **subordinate** clause cannot stand alone; it must be joined with an independent clause to become a sentence.
  because Brian teaches German

- A **phrase** is a group of words that does not have a subject or verb.
  in the beginning of the play

- A **sentence fragment** is not a complete sentence because it lacks a subject or verb or both. It is a phrase or a dependent clause.
  Arrived at the airport just in time.
  Jerry and the adorable spaniel.

- A **run-on sentence** is two or more independent clauses joined incorrectly.
  The rocket ship liftoff failed it had been left unattended for too long.

These are some examples of sentence errors:

Sentence Error	Complete Sentence
To begin the day together.	The class met to begin the day together.
After the band began to play	After the band began to play, my mood improved.
Most of the town's citizens wanted to vote they were eager to be part of the process.	Most of the town's citizens wanted to vote; they were eager to be part of the process.

DIRECTIONS
Read these sentences. Think will help you answer each question.

1. Are some of the most amazing creatures in the world. 2. My adorable cat, for example.

1. Why is sentence 1 an incomplete sentence?

　A. It has no predicate.

　B. It has no subject.

　C. It is an independent clause.

　D. It is a run-on sentence.

Think

1. Reread the question. What is it about?

　Think It is a question about an incomplete sentence.

2. What must you do to answer the question?

　Think I must figure out which answer choice explains why the sentence is incomplete.

3. Try out each answer choice.

　Think The sentence does have a predicate containing a verb. It is not an independent clause because independent clauses can stand on their own as complete sentences. It is not a run-on sentence because two thoughts are not joined incorrectly. There is no subject showing who or what the sentence is about.

4. Choose the BEST answer.

　Think Answer B is the best answer.

2. Which of the following BEST describes sentence 2?

　A. an independent clause

　B. a predicate phrase

　C. a subject

　D. a dependent clause

Think

1. Reread the question. What is it about?

　Think It is a question about the best description of the sentence.

2. What must you do to answer the question?

　Think I must remember the parts of a sentence.

3. Try out each answer choice.

　Think The sentence is not an *independent clause* because it is not a complete thought. It is not a *predicate phrase* or a *dependent clause* because there is no verb. It is a noun phrase, which makes up the subject of a sentence.

4. Choose the best answer.

　Think Answer C is the best answer.

DIRECTIONS
Read this paragraph. Then circle the best answer to each question below. The hints can help you find the correct answers.

(1) Because last month the entire tenth grade got the flu. (2) For nearly two weeks, a large percentage of the class was absent each day. (3) Even the music instructor Mrs. Fleming. (4) When the month finally came to an end.

1. How can you make sentence 1 correct?

A. Add an independent clause.

B. Add a dependent clause.

C. Add a verb phrase.

D. It is correct as is.

Hint   Why can the sentence not stand alone?

2. How should sentence 2 be written correctly?

A. For nearly two weeks, a large percentage of the class.

B. For nearly two weeks, was absent each day.

C. A large percentage of the class for nearly two weeks.

D. It is correct as is.

Hint   Find the subject and predicate and determine whether the sentence can stand alone.

3. How would you correct sentence 3?

A. Add a run-on sentence.

B. Add a predicate.

C. Add an independent clause.

D. It is correct as is.

Hint   *Mrs. Fleming* is the subject. What should be added to tell what happens to her?

4. How could sentence 4 be written correctly?

A. When the month finally came to an end and people got better.

B. When the month finally came to an end and the flu.

C. When the month finally came to an end, we were relieved.

D. It is correct as is.

Hint   The sentence must have a noun that serves as the subject and a verb that serves as the predicate.

5. Rewrite these sentences so that each sentence is complete.

Bali, an island located in Indonesia. Because it is uniquely beautiful, visit each year.

_____

_____

_____

Step 2

A sentence must always have a subject and a verb that can stand alone as a complete thought.

Here are some additional sentence rules:

- In sentences that give orders or instructions, the implied subject of the sentence is *you*.
  (You) Take the garbage to the backyard.

- In questions, the subject usually comes after the verb.
  Did the *trampoline* arrive in the mail?

- The words *there* and *here* are never the subjects of a sentence.
  There *she* is!

Here are some more examples of incomplete sentences.

Incomplete Sentence	Complete Sentence
Why can't win the game?	Why can't we win the game?
Here are.	Here are the Muellers.

DIRECTIONS
Read the story. Use the Reading Guide for tips. Then answer the questions on the next page.

Choosing a Cell Phone

(1) Esther desperately to get a new cell phone. (2) Her old one was beginning to wear out it often made fuzzy sounds while she was talking. (3) Knew she would have to use her own money to upgrade to a new phone. (4) As a result, she was doing a lot of research. (5) She wanted to find the best phone for the best deal.

(6) First, Esther visited some consumer sites online to see what other people said about phones. (7) She also several friends and family members to find out what they liked or didn't like about their phones. (8) Did have particular recommendations for her?

(9) Finally, Esther went to the phone store and talked to the salesperson. (10) Who gave her the information about minutes and cost. (11) When Esther finally made her choice. (12) She was proud of herself. (13) She had spent a little money, but she was confident that she had used that money wisely.

Reading Guide

What is the mistake in sentence 3?

....

What sentence rule is not followed in sentence 7? How would you correct it?

....

Why is sentence 11 not a complete sentence?

Lesson 6: Step 2

DIRECTIONS
Use the passage on the previous page to answer the questions below. Circle the letter beside the correct answer. The hints can help you find the correct answers.

1. How would you correct sentence 1?

   A. Add the verb *wanted.*

   B. Change *Esther* to *She.*

   C. Change *desperately* to *desperate.*

   D. It is correct as is.

   Hint Look for the predicate in the sentence.

2. What is the problem with sentence 2?

   A. It has no predicate.

   B. It has no subject.

   C. It is an independent clause.

   D. It is a run-on sentence.

   Hint Is there a subject and verb in the sentence that creates a complete thought? If so, are there too many subjects and verbs without proper punctuation?

3. How should sentence 8 be correctly written?

   A. Have particular recommendations for her?

   B. Did they have particular recommendations for her?

   C. Particular recommendations for her?

   D. It is correct as is.

   Hint Even questions must have subjects and verbs. Usually subjects come after the verbs in questions—is there one here?

4. Which of the following BEST describes sentence 10?

   A. It is an independent clause.

   B. It is a predicate phrase.

   C. It is a subject.

   D. It is a dependent clause.

   Hint Why can this sentence not stand alone?

5. On the lines below, rewrite the last paragraph of the passage so that all the sentences are complete.

Step 3

DIRECTIONS
Read the article on electronic sound, and then answer the questions below.

Making Electronic Sound

(1) Do know how an electric guitar makes the sounds you enjoy in your music? (2) Read on to find out more about electronic sound.

(3) An electric guitar does not actually make much sound of its own. (4) Instead, electricity makes what you hear when you listen to your favorite bass guitarist. (5) When the metal strings of the guitar are plucked. (6) They vibrate. (7) Then the vibrations become electrical signals. (8) These signals are amplified and turned into sounds that you recognize. (9) Musical artists can also use the processor that amplifies the sound to add certain effects. (10) Including echoing sounds, fuzzing sounds, or other distortions. (11) That is why electric guitars can make sounds that acoustic guitars cannot.

Circle the letter of the best answer.

1. What is one way to correct sentence 1?

   A. Do know how an electric guitar makes the sounds?

   B. You enjoy in your music?

   C. Do you know how an electric guitar makes the sounds you enjoy in your music?

   D. It is correct as is.

2. What is the subject of sentence 2?

   A. read

   B. you

   C. more

   D. sound

3. What is one way to correct sentence 5?

   A. Combine it with sentence 6.

   B. Add a verb phrase.

   C. Divide it into two sentences.

   D. It is correct as is.

4. Which of the following BEST describes sentence 10?

   A. an independent clause

   B. a phrase

   C. a subject

   D. a dependent clause

DIRECTIONS
Read the story. Use the Reading Guide for tips that can help you identify sentence errors as you read. Then answer the questions on the next page.

adapted and excerpted from

How to Cook Fish

By Myrtle Reed

"The Catching of Unshelled Fish"

(1) It is proper, in a treatise devoted entirely to the cooking of unshelled fish, to pay passing attention to the catching. (2) As it is evident that the catching must, in every case precede the cooking. (3) The preface is the place to begin.

(4) Shell-fish are, comparatively, slow of movement, without guile, pitifully trusting. (5) And very easily caught. (6) Observe the difference between the chunk of mutton and four feet of string with which one goes crabbing, and the complicated hooks, rods, flies, and reels devoted to the capture of unshelled fish.

(7) An unshelled fish is lively and elusive past the power of words to portray, in this lies its desirability. (8) People will travel for two nights and a day to some spot where unshelled fish has once been seen, rent a canoe, hire a guide at more than human life is worth in courts of law, and work with dogged patience from gray dawn till sunset. (9) And for what? (10) For one small bass which could have been bought at any trustworthy market for sixty-five cents.

(11) Other fish who have just been weaned. (12) Will repeatedly take a hook too large to swallow, and be dragged into the boat, literally, by the skin of the teeth.

(13) But, as Grover Cleveland said: "He is no true fisherman who is willing to fish only when fish are biting." (14) The real angler will sit all day in a boat in a pouring rain. (15) Eagerly watching the point of the rod, which never for an instant swerves a half inch from the horizontal. (16) The real angler will troll for miles with a hand line and a spinner, winding in the thirty-five dripping feet of the lure every ten minutes, to remove a weed, or "to see if she's still a-spinnin'." (17) Vainly he hopes for the muskellunge who has just gone somewhere else. (18) By the same token, the sure-enough angler is ready to go out next morning, rain or shine, at sunrise.

Reading Guide

What is the problem in sentence 1, if any?

....

How might you fix sentence 5?

....

How would you describe sentence 10?

....

How would you correct sentence 12?

....

What rule is broken in sentence 15?

DIRECTIONS
Now read each question. Circle the letter of the best answer.

1. What is the problem with sentence 2?

    A. It has no predicate.

    B. It has no subject.

    C. It is a dependent clause.

    D. It is a run-on sentence.

    Hint Remember that a clause can have a subject and a predicate without being a complete sentence.

2. What is the subject of sentence 6?

    A. difference

    B. chunk

    C. you

    D. mutton

    Hint Does this sentence give orders or instructions? What rule applies?

3. Which of the following BEST describes sentence 7?

    A. It is a run-on sentence.

    B. It is a predicate phrase.

    C. It is a subject.

    D. It is a dependent clause.

    Hint There is more than one independent clause in this sentence.

4. How would you correct sentence 11?

    A. Add a subject.

    B. Add punctuation.

    C. Add a predicate.

    D. It is correct as is.

    Hint What does this sentence need to be a complete thought?

5. What correction should be made to sentence 18?

    A. Add a subject.

    B. Add a conjunction.

    C. Add a dependent clause.

    D. It is correct as is.

    Hint Is the sentence a complete thought? Can you identify the subject and predicate?

DIRECTIONS
Read this excerpt from *The Wind in the Willows*. Then answer the questions on the next page.

adapted and excerpted from

The Wind in the Willows

by Kenneth Grahame

(1) The Mole had been working very hard all the morning, spring-cleaning his little home. (2) Spring was moving in the air above and in the earth below and around him. (3) It was small wonder, then, that he suddenly flung down his brush on the floor, said "Bother!" and "Hang spring-cleaning!" and bolted out of the house without even waiting to put on his coat. (4) Something up above was calling him he made for the steep little tunnel which answered in his case to the graveled carriage-drive owned by animals whose residences are nearer to the sun and air. (5) So he scraped and scratched and scrabbled and scrooged and then he scrooged again and scrabbled and scratched and scraped. (6) Until at last his snout came out into the sunlight. (7) And he found himself rolling in the warm grass of a great meadow.

(8) "This is fine!" he said to himself. (9) "This is better than whitewashing!" (10) The sunshine struck hot on his fur soft breezes caressed his heated brow. (11) After the seclusion of the cellarage he had lived in so long. (12) The carol of happy birds fell on his dulled hearing almost like a shout. (13) Jumping off all his four legs at once, in the joy of living and the delight of spring without its cleaning, he pursued his way across the meadow till he reached the hedge on the further side.

(14) It all seemed too good to be true. (15) Hither and thither through the meadows he rambled busily. (16) Finding everywhere birds building, flowers budding, leaves thrusting— everything happy, and progressive, and occupied. (17) Instead of having an uneasy conscience pricking him and whispering "whitewash." (18) He somehow could only feel how jolly it was to be the only idle dog among all these busy citizens. (19) After all, the best part of a holiday is perhaps not so much to be resting yourself. (20) As to see all the other fellows busy working.

DIRECTIONS
Read each question. Circle the letter of the best answer.

1. What is the problem with sentence 4?

   A. It has no predicate.

   B. It has no subject.

   C. It is an independent clause.

   D. It is a run-on sentence.

2. Which of the following BEST describes sentence 6?

   A. It is an independent clause.

   B. It is a phrase.

   C. It is a subject.

   D. It is a dependent clause.

3. How might you correct sentence 10?

   A. Put a semicolon after *fur.*

   B. Put a comma after *fur.*

   C. Put *and* after *fur.*

   D. It is correct as is.

4. What is the problem with sentence 11?

   A. The sentence includes no nouns.

   B. The sentence includes no verbs.

   C. It is a dependent clause with no independent clause.

   D. It is correct as is.

5. What is the subject of sentence 12?

   A. carol

   B. birds

   C. hearing

   D. shout

6. Which of the following is a *phrase* from sentence 13?

   A. jumping off all his four legs

   B. in the joy of living

   C. he pursued his way

   D. he reached the hedge

7. What is the main verb in sentence 14?

   A. *seemed*

   B. *good*

   C. *to be*

   D. *true*

8. On a separate sheet of paper, rewrite paragraph 3, fixing all errors.

Lesson 7 • Types of Sentences

Different **types of sentences** have different purposes. Writers use various sentence types to help them convey their ideas most effectively.

The types of sentences:

- A **declarative sentence** makes a statement and ends with a period.
  The Prince of Wales made a television appearance.

- An **interrogative sentence** asks a question and ends with a question mark.
  Why did the battery not charge overnight?

- An **imperative sentence** gives a command or instruction and ends with a period.
  Add some more oregano to the soup.

- An **exclamatory sentence** expresses strong feelings and ends with an exclamation point.
  What an amazing catch Jonathan made!

- A **simple sentence** contains one independent clause—a subject and predicate that can stand alone.
  Charmayne tripped over the thick log.

- A **compound sentence** contains more than one independent clause separated by a semicolon or a comma followed by a conjunction.
  Dan drove the jeep down the muddy road to our campsite, and he discovered it was the wrong road.

- A **complex sentence** contains one independent clause and one or more dependent clauses.
  While you were away, I bought a new car.

- A **compound-complex sentence** contains more than one main clause and at least one dependent clause.
  When Casey came up to bat, the bases were loaded, and there were two outs.

Here are some common errors in sentence-writing.

Sentence Error	Correct Sentence
Bring me the waxed paper for the cookies?	Bring me the waxed paper for the cookies.
That mystery novel, sounds fascinating.	That mystery novel sounds fascinating.
After the party came to an end; the crowd left quickly.	After the party came to an end, the crowd left quickly.

DIRECTIONS
Read these sentences. Think will help you answer each question.

(1) Early humans did not have a written language. (2) Although they were able to communicate, they did it through spoken language.

1. What type of sentence is sentence 1?

   A. declarative

   B. interrogative

   C. imperative

   D. exclamatory

2. Which of the following describes sentence 2?

   A. simple sentence

   B. compound sentence

   C. complex sentence

   D. compound-complex sentence

Think

1. **Reread the question. What is it about?**
   Think It is a question about the type of sentence.

2. **What must you do to answer the question?**
   Think I must figure out which answer choice contains the type of sentence.

3. **Try out each answer choice.**
   Think This sentence does not ask a question, give a command, or state something with great emotion. The sentence makes a statement. Therefore, the sentence must be *declarative*.

4. **Choose the BEST answer.**
   Think Answer A is the best answer.

Think

1. **Reread the question. What is it about?**
   Think It is a question about sentence types.

2. **What must you do to answer the question?**
   Think I must remember the definition of each of these types of sentences.

3. **Try out each answer choice.**
   Think A *simple sentence* has one subject and one predicate. A *compound sentence* has two or more independent clauses. A *complex sentence* has one independent clause and at least one dependent clause. A *compound-complex* sentence has more than one main clause as well as at least one dependent clause. This sentence contains one main clause and one dependent clause.

4. **Choose the BEST answer.**
   Think Answer C is the best answer.

DIRECTIONS
Read this paragraph. Then circle the best answer to each question below.

(1) Until we are able to create more public awareness, our community will not appreciate the importance of using less energy, and the supply will decrease. (2) Did you realize that only a few changes in your household can decrease your energy consumption by a lot. (3) We are starting a group to publicize energy-saving tips we have recruited some people. (4) Consider attending the organizational meeting to find out more information.

1. Which of the following describes sentence 1?

   A. simple sentence

   B. compound sentence

   C. complex sentence

   D. compound-complex sentence

   Hint What subjects and predicates does the sentence contain? Do they stand alone or are they dependent?

2. How would you correct sentence 2?

   A. Change the period to a question mark.

   B. Add a subject to the sentence.

   C. Add a period after *household.*

   D. It is correct as is.

   Hint Consider the type of the sentence and its purpose. What mistake has been made?

3. How should sentence 3 be written correctly?

   A. We are starting a group to publicize energy-saving tips, we have recruited some people.

   B. We are starting a group to publicize energy-saving tips, and we have recruited some people.

   C. We are starting a group to publicize energy-saving tips; and we have recruited some people.

   D. It is correct as is.

   Hint How should the two independent clauses of a compound sentence be joined?

4. What type of sentence is sentence 4?

   A. declarative

   B. interrogative

   C. imperative

   D. exclamatory

   Hint What is the purpose of the sentence?

5. Rewrite these sentences so that each sentence is correct.

   Each year I make new resolutions? I make a lot of promises. I rarely keep them.

Each sentence type serves a different purpose. Writers should be able to use all sentence types in order to convey their ideas clearly and concisely.

Here are some additional rules about sentence type in writing:

- Use varying sentence types within a piece of writing.

- Punctuate all sentences correctly in order to convey ideas clearly.

- Be sure the sentence type matches your purpose. For example, if you want to convey excitement, be sure to use an exclamatory sentence.

- Combine sentences to make a new sentence type to improve the flow of ideas.
  Sal ordered the new saw from the factory. He ordered the new drill, as well.
  (two simple sentences)
  Improved: When Sal ordered the new saw, he also ordered the new drill.
  (complex sentence)

Here are some more common errors in sentence-writing.

Sentence	Improved Sentence
Get out of the way, you might get hurt.	Get out of the way, or you might get hurt!
We traveled across the Mississippi River. Then we traveled up the Missouri River. Finally we traveled into Minnesota.	We traveled across the Mississippi River, up the Missouri River, and finally into Minnesota.

DIRECTIONS
Read the story. Use the Reading Guide for tips. Then answer the questions on the next page.

Coral Reefs

(1) Many people appreciate the importance of the coral reef in the life of the ocean. (2) The largest reef in the world is the Great Barrier Reef in Australia. (3) Within these reefs colorful fish swim. (4) Shrimps hide for safety. (5) Sea horses anchor their bodies to the coral.

(6) But did you, realize that coral reefs are also dangerous. (7) Although coral reefs provide hiding places for small sea life, many predators know this. (8) An octopus might lurk within a coral reef; he comes out when his prey swims near.

(9) Sea anemones also live in corals. (10) They are dangerous. (11) They have poisonous tentacles. (12) Some corals are even poisonous themselves. (13) These stinging corals can even harm humans who touch them. (14) Remember to be careful if you ever swim near a reef?

Reading Guide

What type of sentence is sentence 4—declarative or imperative?

....

Is sentence 7 a compound sentence or a complex sentence?

....

How can you tell sentence 14 should be an imperative sentence?

DIRECTIONS
Use the passage on the previous page to answer the questions below. Circle the letter beside the correct answer. The hints can help you find the correct answers.

1. What type of sentence is sentence 1?

   A. simple sentence

   B. compound sentence

   C. complex sentence

   D. compound-complex sentence

   Hint Look for the subject and the predicate of the sentence. Are there more than one?

2. How could sentences 3, 4, and 5 be combined?

   A. Within these reefs: colorful fish swim; shrimps hide for safety; sea horses anchor their bodies to the coral!

   B. Within these reefs, colorful fish swim, shrimps hide for safety, and horses anchor their bodies to the coral.

   C. Within these reefs colorful fish swim, and shrimps hide for safety, sea horses anchor their bodies to the coral.

   D. They cannot be combined.

   Hint Combine three simple sentences.

3. How should sentence 6 be correctly written?

   A. But did you realize that coral reefs are also dangerous.

   B. But did you realize: that coral reefs are also dangerous!

   C. But did you realize that coral reefs are also dangerous?

   D. It is correct as is.

   Hint What is the author trying to do in this sentence?

4. How could you correct sentence 8?

   A. An octopus might lurk within a coral reef; and then he comes out when his prey swims near.

   B. An octopus might lurk within a coral reef he comes out when his prey swims near.

   C. An octopus might lurk within a coral reef, he comes out when his prey swims near.

   D. It is correct as is.

   Hint How can two independent clauses be joined?

5. On the lines below, rewrite the last paragraph of the passage so that all the sentences are complete. Be sure to combine sentences if it will improve the flow of ideas.

   _____

   _____

   _____

   _____

DIRECTIONS
Read the story, and then answer the questions below.

A Mighty Ruckus

(1) As I rounded the corner of my block, I heard my sister screaming. (2) What could be going on. (3) It did not take me long to recognize a typical family scenario. (4) My younger brother Jack was outside with my sister. (5) My sister was babysitting him. (6) He has this habit of pretending to be a kitten, which is adorable for about five minutes. (7) After he makes kitty sounds for more than that, our nerves begin to fray. (8) My poor sister had already been with him for two hours, and she was desperately waiting for someone to relieve her from her duty.

Circle the letter of the best answer.

1. What type of sentence is sentence 1?

    A. simple sentence

    B. compound sentence

    C. complex sentence

    D. compound-complex sentence

2. How should you correct the mistake in sentence 2?

    A. Change *What* to *How.*

    B. Insert a comma after *What.*

    C. Divide the sentence into two.

    D. Change the period to a question mark.

3. What is the BEST way to combine sentences 4 and 5?

    A. My younger brother Jack was outside with my sister, my sister was babysitting him.

    B. My younger brother Jack was outside with my sister, who was babysitting him.

    C. My younger brother Jack was outside with my sister; and my sister was babysitting him.

    D. They cannot be combined.

4. What part of sentence 7 is the independent clause?

    A. After he makes kitty sounds

    B. kitty sounds

    C. for more than that

    D. our nerves begin to fray

DIRECTIONS
Read the story. Use the Reading Guide for tips that can help you identify sentence errors as you read. Then answer the questions on the next page.

adapted and excerpted from

"Rain"

by W. Somerset Maugham

(1) It was nearly bedtime, and when they awoke next morning, land would be in sight. (2) Dr. Macphail lit his pipe. (3) He searched the heavens for the Southern Cross. (4) After two years at the front and a wound that had taken longer to heal than it should, he was glad to settle down quietly at Apia. (5) He felt already better for the journey. (6) Since some of the passengers were leaving the ship the next day at Pago–Pago, they had had a little dance that evening, and in his ears hammered still the harsh notes of the mechanical piano. (7) But the deck was quiet at last? (8) A little way off he saw his wife in a long chair talking with the Davidsons, and he strolled over to her.

(9) He had very red hair. (10) He had a bald patch on the crown and red, freckled skin. (11) He was a man of forty and thin. (12) He had a pinched face. (13) He spoke with a Scots accent in a very low, quiet voice.

(14) Between the Macphails and the Davidsons there had arisen the intimacy of shipboard, which is due to nearness rather than to any community of taste. (15) Their chief tie was the disapproval they shared of the other men. (16) Mrs. Macphail was flattered she realized she and her husband were the only people with whom the Davidsons were willing to associate. (17) Even the doctor half unconsciously acknowledged the compliment. (18) Because he was of an argumentative mind, he permitted himself to complain in their cabin at night.

Reading Guide

What type of sentence is sentence 1?

....

What is the independent clause in sentence 4?

....

What is the error in sentence 7?

....

What type of corrections might you make to paragraph 2?

....

What is the purpose of the declarative sentence 17?

.

DIRECTIONS
Now read each question. Circle the letter of the best answer.

1. How could you combine sentences 2 and 3 to make a compound sentence?

    A. Dr. Macphail lit his pipe, he searched the heavens for the Southern Cross.

    B. Dr. Macphail lit his pipe, and he searched the heavens for the Southern Cross.

    C. Dr. Macphail lit his pipe he searched the heavens for the Southern Cross.

    D. They cannot be combined.

    Hint What is the rule for combining independent clauses?

2. What type of sentence is sentence 6?

    A. simple sentence

    B. compound sentence

    C. complex sentence

    D. compound-complex sentence

    Hint Look for the subject and the predicate of the sentence. Are there more than one?

3. What is the main problem in paragraph 2?

    A. The questions do not have question marks.

    B. The subject is unclear.

    C. All the sentences are the same type.

    D. There is no problem.

    Hint Think about the characteristics of good writing. What types of sentences should be used?

4. How should sentence 16 be written correctly?

    A. Mrs. Macphail was flattered, she realized she and her husband were the only people with whom the Davidsons were willing to associate.

    B. Mrs. Macphail was flattered; she realized she and her husband were the only people with whom the Davidsons were willing to associate.

    C. Mrs. Macphail was flattered, realized she and her husband were the only people with whom the Davidsons were willing to associate.

    D. It is correct as is.

    Hint The sentence has two independent clauses. How should they be joined?

5. What is the dependent clause in sentence 18?

    A. Because he was of an argumentative mind

    B. he permitted himself

    C. to complain in their cabin at night

    D. There is no dependent clause.

    Hint A dependent clause cannot stand alone, but it does have a subject and a verb.

DIRECTIONS
Read this sample student essay about castles. Then answer the questions on the next page.

What Are Castles?

(1) Castles seem to have always captured the imaginations of young people. (2) What child does not enjoy a fairy tale which includes a castle, and some royal princes or princesses. (3) Tourists visit castles all over Europe. (4) Toy makers make plastic castles for children to play with. (5) Hotels refurbish castles, renting out the rooms at high prices. (6) But in their day, castles were probably not as glamorous as they seem to us today. (7) Castles served a very practical purpose and probably saved the lives of thousands of people.

(8) You might think castles were simply fancy houses for rich people. (9) You are quite wrong. (10) Castles were actually military and civil fortifications. (11) The castles protected the people within from the warring forces on the outside. (12) Much of the castle interior was not used for living space. (13) Instead, it housed guards. (14) It housed meeting rooms. (15) Perhaps it even housed a dungeon with cells for prisoners.

(16) Castles included much more than the turreted building itself. (17) The main building was typically made of stone or wood. (18) An outer wall of stone or timber encircled the castle and its grounds. (19) The wall included towers where guards could survey what was going on beyond. (20) When they spotted trouble, they sent out warnings and responded to the situation. (21) Sometimes a moat surrounded the wall for added protection. (22) To get into the castle grounds, people (and animals) entered through a drawbridge, which was a hinged door that folded down and up.

(23) Within the walls were other necessary buildings? (24) When an enemy attacked. (25) Villagers could stay sheltered within the castle walls. (26) Many castles had their own churches or chapels. (27) The inner side of the wall provided stable areas for the horses and other animals gardens provided food for the castle dwellers.

DIRECTIONS
Now read each question. Circle the letter of the best answer.

1. How should sentence 2 be written correctly?

   A. What child does not enjoy a fairy tale; which includes a castle, and some royal princes or princesses.

   B. What child does not enjoy a fairy tale, which includes a castle, and some royal princes, or princesses.

   C. What child does not enjoy a fairy tale which includes a castle and some royal princes or princesses?

   D. It is correct as is.

2. How would you combine sentences 8 and 9 to make them into a complex sentence?

   A. You might think castles were simply fancy houses for rich people, but you are quite wrong?

   B. You might think castles were simply fancy houses for rich people you are quite wrong.

   C. You might think castles were simply fancy houses for rich people, and you are quite wrong.

   D. If you think castles were simply fancy houses for rich people, you are quite wrong.

3. If sentences 3, 4, and 5 are combined, what type of sentence would it be?

   A. simple

   B. compound

   C. complex

   D. compound-complex

4. What type of sentence is sentence 18?

   A. simple sentence

   B. compound sentence

   C. complex sentence

   D. compound-complex sentence

5. What is the dependent clause in sentence 20?

   A. When they spotted trouble

   B. they sent out warnings

   C. and responded

   D. to the situation

6. Which of the following is an imperative sentence you could add to the end of the essay?

   A. Do you want to find out more about castles?

   B. I think castles are absolutely fascinating!

   C. Go to your local library if you want to learn more about castles.

   D. Castles were first built in Europe in the 8th century.

7. On a separate sheet of paper, rewrite paragraph 4 fixing all errors.

Lesson 8 • Sentence Structure

Strong **sentence structure** holds a piece of writing together by giving it force and interest.

Here are some key rules for writing strong sentences:

- Use clear, concise sentences rather than wordy or repetitive sentences.
  Wordy: That letter that I sent to the editor who is in charge of the newspaper had a lot of my ideas in it and I thought they were very clear.
  Concise: My letter to the newspaper editor expressed my ideas clearly.

- Use **parallel structures** to express equal ideas and keep similar parts of a sentence in the same form so that the reader can see that they form a connected list of words or phrases.
  Not Parallel: When I go on vacation, I like <u>to shop</u>, <u>to fish</u>, and <u>going to the beach.</u>
  Parallel: When I go on vacation, I like <u>to shop</u>, <u>to fish</u>, and <u>to go</u> to the beach.

- Vary your sentence beginnings.
  Weak: The band began to play a Sousa march. The audience seemed to respond. Children started to dance around the room. Parents tapped their feet along with the music and laughed.
  Stronger: When the band began to play a Sousa march, the audience seemed to respond. Children started to dance around the room. Laughing, parents tapped their feet along with the music.

- Use active rather than passive voice in most of your writing.
  Passive: Casey was thrown into the water when the jet ski suddenly stopped.
  Active: Casey catapulted into the water when the jet ski suddenly stopped.

Here are some common weaknesses in sentence structure:

Poor Sentence Structure	Improved Sentence Structure
Would you consider doing me the favor of attending my graduation party?	Would you come to my graduation party?
Some of Margarita's favorite hobbies are swimming, painting, and to read.	Some of Margarita's favorite hobbies are swimming, painting, and reading.

DIRECTIONS
Read these sentences. Think will help you answer each question.

(1) This morning Mom asked me whether I preferred dancing, writing, or to act.

(2) The answer was not known to me.

1. What is the main problem with sentence 1?

    A. It is in the passive voice.

    B. It uses complicated words.

    C. It is not a complete sentence.

    D. It is not parallel.

2. What would be the BEST way to improve sentence 2?

    A. Use simpler words.

    B. Make it active voice.

    C. Use more words.

    D. Make it parallel.

Think

1. Reread the question. What is it about?

    Think It is a question about a problem in the first sentence.

2. What must you do to answer the question?

    Think I must figure out which answer choice best describes the main weakness of the sentence.

3. Try out each answer choice.

    Think The sentence is not in the *passive voice*. There are no *complicated words* in the sentence. It is a *complete sentence*. The final part of the sentence—*dancing, writing, and to act*—contains equal ideas, but they are not expressed in the same way. The words *to act* should be *acting*.

4. Choose the BEST answer.

    Think Answer D is the best answer.

Think

1. Reread the question. What is it about?

    Think It is a question about a weak sentence.

2. What must you do to answer the question?

    Think I must remember the rules of strong sentence structure.

3. Try out each answer choice.

    Think The sentence already contains *simple words*. *More words* would not necessarily improve this sentence because the problem is related to its structure. There are no ideas that need to be *made parallel*. Instead, the sentence is passive—the subject *answer* is not doing the action. This makes a sentence weak.

4. Choose the BEST answer.

    Think Answer B is the best answer.

DIRECTIONS
Read this paragraph. Then circle the best answer to each question below. The hints can help you find the correct answers.

(1) The best crab cakes in the world are made by my grandmother. (2) She has been mixing, shaping, and to fry them for at least fifty years. (3) Each of the bites of her crab cakes does taste quite nice in the mouth because they have good flavor. (4) My dad agrees that grandmother should win a culinary prize for her recipe.

1. How should sentence 1 be written?

 A. The tastiest crab cakes in the world are created by my grandma.

 B. My grandmother makes the best crab cakes in the world.

 C. The most delectable crab cakes are constructed by my mother's mother, who is my grandmother.

 D. It is correct as is.

 Hint   Which sentence is most direct?

2. How would you correct sentence 2?

 A. Change *to fry* to *frying.*

 B. Change *mixing* to *mix.*

 C. Change *years* to *12-month cycles.*

 D. It is correct as is.

 Hint   Are similar ideas presented in the same way?

3. How could sentence 3 be revised?

 A. Every single one of the bites of her crab cakes tastes so nice in the mouth because they are flavorful.

 B. The individual bites of her crab cakes have a nice flavor and taste good when you eat them.

 C. Each flavorful bite tastes delicious.

 D. It is correct as is.

 Hint   This sentence has too many words. Which revision makes it clear and concise?

4. Which of the following would improve the whole paragraph?

 A. Make all the sentences passive.

 B. Vary the sentence beginnings.

 C. Use fewer complicated words.

 D. Combine all the sentences into one.

 Hint   Look at the paragraph as a whole. How could it be improved to make it more interesting?

5. Rewrite this sentence to make it stronger.

The mountaineer tried to move from the blizzard that threatened to trap him in deep snow, far from any other humans where he might get stuck and not find people to help him.

_____

_____

_____

Step 2

Writers use strong sentence structure to convey ideas clearly and precisely. They do this by using concise and active language. They also use a variety of sentence types to keep readers from getting bored.

Here are some additional ideas for creating strong sentence structure:

- Create variety by using **gerunds**, **participles**, and **infinitives.**
  Gerund: <u>Camping</u> teaches young people the value of hard work.
  Participle: <u>Calling loudly to his uncle,</u> Malcolm announced the arrival of the ice cream truck.
  Infinitive: She asked <u>to go</u> to the spring festival next weekend.

- Avoid **dangling** and **misplaced modifiers.**
  Incorrect: Eager to find a drink to quench his thirst, the bottle of juice was a welcome surprise.
  Correct: Eager to find a drink to quench his thirst, the man was surprised to find the bottle of juice.

DIRECTIONS
Read the story. Use the Reading Guide for tips. Then answer the questions on the next page.

Lab Safety

(1) Most high school students are required by state law to take several science classes before they graduate. (2) For many of these students, the part they like most, the most enjoyable feature of science class is working in a lab. (3) But before working in any lab, the rules of safety must be learned by students.

(4) One important rule is to wear safety goggles. (5) Another rule is to wear clothing that covers the arms, legs, body, and feet. (6) Most labs also provide lab aprons or coats. (7) Students should tie back long hair so that it does not get in the way. (8) Eating, drinking, and to smoke are always prohibited in laboratories.

(9) Laboratories often contain chemicals and flames, which are used to do experiments and other stuff like that which might be done in a science situation. (10) Always use caution when you are around chemicals and flames. (11) A good rule to follow is to be more careful than you think you need to be.

Reading Guide

What is the problem with sentence 2?

....

How do all the sentences in paragraph 2 begin?

....

How could you rewrite sentence 9 to strengthen it?

DIRECTIONS
Use the passage on the previous page to answer the questions below. Circle the letter beside the correct answer. The hints can help you find the correct answers.

1. What makes sentence 1 a weak sentence?

   A. It does not use parallel structure.

   B. It has complicated language.

   C. It is in passive voice.

   D. It is not weak.

   Hint Is the subject doing the action or is the action being done to the subject?

2. Which of the following BEST improves sentence 3?

   A. But before working in any lab, students must learn the rules of safety.

   B. But before working in any lab, safety rules must be learned by students.

   C. The rules of safety must be learned by students before working in any lab.

   D. It is correct as is.

   Hint This sentence has a misplaced modifer *and* passive voice.

3. How could sentence 7 be rewritten so that it does not begin with the subject of the sentence?

   A. To prevent hair from getting in the way, students should tie back long hair.

   B. Tying back long hair keeps it out of the way.

   C. Long hair should be tied back so that it does not get in the way.

   D. Students should consider tying back long hair to keep it out of the way.

   Hint A subject is the noun that states who or what the sentence is about.

4. How would you correct sentence 8?

   A. Eating, to drink, and to smoke are always prohibited in laboratories.

   B. Always prohibited in laboratories are: eating, drinking, and to smoke.

   C. Eating, drinking, and smoking are always prohibited in laboratories.

   D. Laboratories prohibit eating, drinking, and to smoke.

   Hint The list of activities needs to be presented in parallel form.

5. On the lines below, rewrite the second paragraph of the passage to make it stronger.

   _____

   _____

   _____

   _____

Step 3

DIRECTIONS
Read the passage, and then answer the questions below.

Tiling Surfaces

(1) Many people use linoleum tile on their kitchen floors. (2) But my dad is convinced that ceramic tile creates a more beautiful and durable surface. (3) Linoleum tiles are dirtied more easily because of the material. (4) This might be true, I think, because dirt does show up at my grandmother's house, and she has linoleum on her floor, although she does not have a lot of time for cleaning either. (5) Dad is not insistent that everyone use ceramic tile. (6) But he does encourage people to research, touch, and viewing ceramic tiles before making a decision.

Circle the letter of the best answer.

1. How could sentences 1 and 2 be combined to make a sentence that does not begin with the subject?

    A. Many people use linoleum tile on their kitchen floors, my dad is convinced that ceramic tile creates a more beautiful and durable surface.

    B. My dad is convinced that ceramic tile creates a more beautiful and durable surface even though many people use linoleum tile on their kitchen floors.

    C. Kitchen floors should be tiled with ceramic rather than linoleum, according to my dad.

    D. Although many people use linoleum tile on their kitchen floors, my dad is convinced that ceramic tile creates a more beautiful and durable surface.

2. What would be the BEST way to improve sentence 4?

    A. use fewer words

    B. make it active voice

    C. use more words

    D. make it parallel

3. What is the correct way to write sentence 6?

    A. But he does encourage people to researching, touching, and viewing ceramic tiles before making a decision.

    B. But he does encouraging people to research, touch, and viewing ceramic tiles before make a decision.

    C. But he does encourage people to research, touch, and view ceramic tiles before making a decision.

    D. It is correct as is.

DIRECTIONS
Read the story. Use the Reading Guide for tips that can help you identify weak sentences as you read. Then answer the questions on the next page.

Malawi

(1) Humans lived in what is now the country of Malawi as early as 8000 BC. (2) Various tribal kingdoms dwelled in the region for thousands of years. (3) No central government ruled the area until the British arrived. (4) In 1964, the country of Malawi, which had controlled the area since 1891, gained independence from the United Kingdom. (5) Not until 1993, however, did the Malawian people vote to become a multiparty democracy. (6) Between 1964 and 1994, the country was ruled by a dictator. (7) He wanted to stay president for life.

(8) Malawi is located in southeastern Africa, where it borders the countries of Tanzania, Mozambique, and Zambia. (9) The country is landlocked, surrounded by land, which means that it does not have any coasts on oceans, and that there is no water from the sea that comes up next to the border. (10) There are significant bodies of water within Malawi, however, including Lake Malawi, one of the largest lakes on the continent. (11) Lake Malawi lies within the Great Rift Valley, which cuts north and south up this region of the continent. (12) Several important rivers in Malawi are the Shire and the Zambezi.

(13) Maize is the main food staple in Malawi, a corn product. (14) But famines are not unusual in Malawi. (15) Many of the country's people suffer from hunger and malnutrition. (16) Many people live only on the food they make, so a drought or flooding is equally devastating.

(17) Tourists travel to Malawi to take in the sights of the natural parks, to visit the game reserves, and hiking the mountains. (18) Most tourists visit during the dry season, between April and October, although the weather can be very hot.

Reading Guide

Is sentence 2 active or passive voice?
....

What is the infinitive in sentence 5?
....

What is the problem in sentence 13?
....

What phrase could you insert so that sentence 15 does not begin with the subject?
....

How could paragraph 3 be improved?

DIRECTIONS
Now read each question. Circle the letter of the best answer.

1. How could sentence 1 be rewritten so it does not begin with the subject?

   A. What is now the country of Malawi has contained humans as early as 8000 BC.

   B. As early as 8000 BC, humans lived in what is now the country of Malawi.

   C. The country of Malawi has held humans since as early as 8000 BC.

   D. Humans lived as early as 8000 BC in what is now the country of Malawi.

   Hint Choose the sentence that does not begin with a noun of any kind.

2. What is wrong with sentence 4?

   A. It is passive voice.

   B. It is not a complete sentence.

   C. There is a misplaced modifier.

   D. It is correct as is.

   Hint Where should the phrase "which had controlled the area since 1891" be placed?

3. How could you correct the mistake in sentence 17?

   A. Split it into two sentences.

   B. Change *hiking* to *to hike.*

   C. Change *Tourists travel to Malawi* to *Malawi is visited by tourists.*

   D. It is correct as is.

   Hint Similar ideas within the sentence should be presented in similar fashion.

4. How would you correct sentence 6?

   A. The country was ruled by a dictator between 1964 and 1994.

   B. A dictator ruled the country between 1964 and 1994.

   C. 1964 and 1994 were the years in which the country was ruled by a dictator.

   D. Between 1964 and 1994, a dictator was ruled by the country.

   Hint Make the sentence stronger by having the subject do the action rather than receive it.

5. What is the BEST way to rewrite sentence 9?

   A. The country is landlocked, which means that it does not have any borders.

   B. The country is landlocked, which means that it is surrounded by land and no water from the sea comes up next to its border.

   C. The landlocked country is, surrounded by land, does not have any coasts on oceans, and there is no water from the sea that comes up next to the border.

   D. The country is surrounded by land, landlocked, there is no water from the sea that comes up next to the border.

   Hint Eliminate unnecessary or repetitive words.

115

DIRECTIONS
Read this sample student essay about a change in eating habits. Then answer the questions on the next page.

Think Before You Eat

(1) Until I was 15 years old, I put very little thinking into the food I ate. (2) I do not mean that I didn't think about food. (3) When I got up in the morning, I wanted to eat. (4) When I got home from school, I had a snack. (5) When I made it to the dinner table, I was fairly drooling.

(6) What I didn't think about was where my food came from. (7) Maybe I assumed that the juicy orange fell from the sky in my refrigerator. (8) I did not care much about what I ate, and I couldn't have cared less about where it originated.

(9) That all changed last summer when I lived with my Aunt Tess on her small farm. (10) At Aunt Tess's, everything that ends up on the dining room table has been thought about. (11) Did the chicken come from a local farmer who raises them in the open? (12) Were the cows fed healthy food? (13) Were they injected with antibiotics? (14) Aunt Tess is committed to local food, so these are very important factors.

(15) She sure does think that if the food a person eats or consumes is going to be local, it also has to be seasonal and fresh to that time of year. (16) That means that even if she is craving asparagus in November, Aunt Tess cannot eat it. (17) In her rural community, asparagus does not grow in November; it grows in the spring. (18) So, asparagus is eaten only in spring. (19) She doesn't just eat it, though. (20) The woman relishes it, she savors it, she delighting in it. (21) Then she moves on to the next fresh vegetable and thinks about how she will enjoy asparagus again next year.

(22) The environmental impact of her food is also considered by Aunt Tess. (23) One of the reasons she buys local is because buying from far away uses fuel. (24) The transportation costs for the food are minimal when she eats locally.

(25) I don't think I will ever be as rigorous about my diet as Aunt Tess is. (26) But she is admired by me for her commitment to the environment and to her community. (27) I left her farm. (28) I have changed my own diet. (29) I try to eat local and seasonal foods. (30) I could eat an out-of-season peach from South America. (31) But I choose an apple that was grown in a neighboring township.

DIRECTIONS
Now read each question. Circle the letter of the best answer.

1. Which word BEST describes the structure of sentences 3, 4, and 5?

   A. passive

   B. parallel

   C. incomplete

   D. dangling

2. How should you correct sentence 7?

   A. Maybe I assumed that in my refrigerator the juicy orange fell from the sky.

   B. Maybe I assumed that my refrigerator with the juicy orange fell from the sky.

   C. Maybe I assumed that the juicy orange in my refrigerator fell from the sky.

   D. I assumed that the juicy orange that fell from the sky was maybe in my refrigerator.

3. How could sentence 15 be revised?

   A. If the food a person eats is going to be local, it also has to be seasonal.

   B. She strongly believes that if the food a person eats or consumes is going to be local, it also has to be seasonal and fresh.

   C. Some people eat local and seasonal food.

   D. Seasonal and fresh food that a person consumes or eats must be local to be at its freshest.

4. How can you make sentence 18 active voice?

   A. So, asparagus is being eaten only in spring.

   B. So, she eats asparagus only in the spring.

   C. So, asparagus is to be eaten only in spring.

   D. Eating asparagus only happens in spring.

5. Which word is incorrect in sentence 20?

   A. woman

   B. relishes

   C. savors

   D. delighting

6. What would be the BEST way to improve sentence 22?

   A. Use simpler words.

   B. Make it active voice.

   C. Use more words.

   D. Make it parallel.

7. On a separate sheet of paper, rewrite the final paragraph. Make the sentences clearer, stronger, and more effective.

Lesson 9 • Persuasive Writing

Prewriting

A writer has a **purpose** in mind each time he or she writes a composition. In **persuasive writing**, the purpose is to convince readers to think a certain way or to take an action. The writer takes a clear position on an issue and presents a logical argument. He or she uses examples, facts, and reasons to support each point of the argument, and closes with a strong restatement or summary of the argument. Types of persuasive writing include persuasive essays, speeches, and letters; newspaper editorials; and reviews.

When writing a persuasive composition, remember to do the following:

- Take one firm position. Think carefully about what it is you want to convince your audience to think or do.

- State your position clearly in the opening of your composition.

- Stay focused on the issue you are writing about and maintain your position throughout the composition.

- Organize your ideas and points in a logical order.

- Use specific reasons, examples, and facts to support your different points and your overall position.

- Examine different perspectives on the issue and consider counter arguments. Respond to these different arguments.

- End with a strong closing. The closing should gather the points of your argument into a clear statement.

- Use correct spelling, punctuation, capitalization, grammar, and sentence structure.

Brainstorming

When students run for office at school, they make speeches to convince listeners about various topics. Imagine you are running for office. What would you want to convince fellow students about? What things at your school should change? Are there problems you think should be fixed?

Brainstorming will help you come up with ideas for a persuasive speech. List ideas for a persuasive speech on the next page.

1. IDEA _____

    _____

2. IDEA _____

    _____

3. IDEA _____

    _____

4. IDEA _____

    _____

Building Ideas

You have generated several ideas for a persuasive speech. Now build on your ideas by adding more thoughts and details. Choose your two best ideas from above. For each idea, think of the clear position you would take and write it below. Then think of the different points you would make to support your position.

Position 1: _____

Supporting points:

    1. _____

    2. _____

    3. _____

    4. _____

Position 2: _____

Supporting points:

    1. _____

    2. _____

    3. _____

    4. _____

Organizing Your Argument

In any persuasive piece, the argument should be easy to follow. It should flow logically from one point to the next. Each point of the argument should be supported with specific examples, details, facts, or reasons. No points should be weak, vague, or off the topic.

DIRECTIONS
Pick one of your ideas from the previous page to write a persuasive speech. Use this graphic organizer to help plot out the structure.

TOPIC: _____

My position:

↓

Main point:

Examples, details, facts, reasons:
_____
_____
_____

↓

Main point:

Examples, details, facts, reasons:
_____
_____
_____

↓

Main point:

Examples, details, facts, reasons:
_____
_____
_____

↓

My conclusion:

Step 2

Drafting

Openings

A strong **opening** captures the audience's attention and interest. When you write a persuasive composition, it is important to state your position clearly in your opening. This will help readers follow your argument and decide how well you support your point of view throughout.

As you prepare to write a draft of a persuasive piece, review these strategies for writing an effective opener:

Strategy	Example
State a fact or opinion.	A large percentage of accidents on the road are caused by teenage drivers.
Use an example.	Late in the evening most nights, Sylvia is slumped over a mountain of homework. Exhausted from a jam-packed schedule, she never finishes her schoolwork until well after midnight.
Use a definition.	Service learning is a strategy many schools use to combine community service and classroom learning. It is a brilliant concept that our own school must embrace.
Challenge your readers.	Everyone at Liberty High School likes our school uniforms, right? It may seem so, but in truth they are highly controversial.

DIRECTIONS
A student wrote a persuasive essay about changing the voting age. Currently, citizens need to be 18 to vote in national elections. This student argued that the voting age should be lowered to 16. Evaluate his opening and write a stronger opening below. Review the strategies above as you write.

> I think it would be interesting if the voting age was the same age for driving a car in most states. That age is 16. Usually people are mature enough at age 16 to handle driving a car, so I don't see why they wouldn't be mature enough at that age to vote in a national election.

_____

_____

_____

_____

_____

Transitions

Smooth **transitions** lead the reader from one point to the next. They connect new ideas to the ideas that came before them. In persuasive writing, a writer adds new ideas with transition words like *also, additionally,* and *in the same way.* The writer shows contrasting ideas with words like *but* and *however.* He or she concludes or sums up a line of reasoning with words such as *consequently, therefore,* and *as a result.*

DIRECTIONS
Read this student's persuasive essay in response to a proposed cell phone ban at her school. Choose the best transition words from the box below to complete her essay.

in the same way	consequently	even worse	next
despite	first	but	additionally

I Need My Cell Phone

In this day and age, communication is everything. New technologies make it easier than ever to converse with one another. (1) _____ what good are these technologies if we're not allowed to use them? Principal Jackson wants to ban us from using cell phones during all school hours. I think this is a terrible idea—and one that will have many negative consequences.

(2) _____ let's consider the basics. Parents communicate with their children through cell phones very frequently these days. They even check in during school hours. If they're picking their son or daughter up and a change of plans occurs, they need to be able to communicate. (3) _____, if a student needs to reach his or her parent about a change of schedule, he or she should be able to make a quick call as soon as possible.

(4) _____, there might someday be a real emergency. This could be a personal emergency in someone's family, or an issue that affects the whole community, such as a weather crisis or even a national disaster.

Some teachers argue that cell phones make distracting noises during school. Others worry that students will use text messaging to cheat on tests. (5) _____, they support Principal Jackson's proposed ban. But solving the noise problem is easy: We can all turn our ringers off or set them on vibrate. To prevent cheating, we should have an honor code among students. (6) _____, teachers should continue to closely monitor students during tests, just as they did before cell phones even existed.

(7) _____ the many arguments against cell phone use in schools, cell phones are a necessity in today's world. It's simply unfair to deprive students of these important communication tools. (8) _____ Principal Jackson will want to ban computers because *they* make noise and can lead to cheating! We students must insist on our right to modern technology and say no to the proposed cell phone ban.

Closings

The **closing** of any composition is the final thought the writer leaves a reader. The closing is the last chance to make an impression or get a message across. A strong closing in a persuasive piece restates the main argument or gathers the points of the argument into a clear statement. It might also use humor to make its point or call for some kind of action. Most importantly, the closing should follow logically from the rest of the piece.

As you prepare to write a draft of a persuasive piece, review these strategies for writing an effective closing:

Strategy	Example
Sum up your argument.	Our school day is simply too long. Students get too exhausted, teachers get too worn out, and our leaning suffers as a whole.
Make a call for action.	All students must speak with a unified voice and protest the new grading system.
Use humor, and/or quotations.	As Yogi Berra said, "It's déjà vu all over again."
Spark your readers' imaginations.	With more money allocated to our sports' teams, every single team could be unstoppable this year.

DIRECTIONS
A student wrote a persuasive essay about the importance of reading books. She argued that teenagers watch far too much TV and read far too few books. Evaluate her closing and write a stronger closing below. Review the strategies above as you write.

As a conclusion, I think books are much more important than TV. I've already written about how teens waste too much time watching TV. And about how so many books out there are truly terrific to read. Just like I said, we would be better off spending more time reading than watching TV.

_____

_____

_____

_____

_____

Drafting

You have generated ideas and reviewed openings, transitions, and closings. Now it is time to write a draft. A **draft** is a chance to get all of your ideas on paper and organize your composition. In writing a persuasive draft, remember to clearly state your position and write out each point of your argument. Support each point with specific examples, facts, details, or reasons, and write a strong closing. In drafting any persuasive piece, make sure to stay focused on the topic and to maintain one clear position.

DIRECTIONS
Use your notes from pages 119 and 120 and what you have learned about openings, transitions, and closings to write a draft of a persuasive speech to the student body. Begin your draft here and continue on a separate sheet of paper if necessary.

Title of Speech: _____

_____

_____

_____

_____

_____

_____

_____

_____

_____

_____

_____

_____

_____

_____

_____

Step 3

Revising and Editing

Once you have written your first draft, you will need to **revise** and **edit**. In the revision process, a writer makes changes to improve his or her composition. Writers review the organization and focus of their draft, and how their ideas are supported. They watch for ways to make their writing more clear. Writers also make edits to correct mistakes in spelling, punctuation, capitalization, grammar, and sentence structure.

DIRECTIONS
Read these paragraphs from a student's persuasive essay about making community service mandatory. Look for ways to improve it, and answer the questions on the following page.

To Serve or Not to Serve

(1) "Its better too give than to recieve." (2) If Wilson High School would adopt a policy of mandatory community service, our students would have the chance to fully understand the meaning behind these words.

(3) Many high schools nationwide wisely require students to spend time serving their community. (4) This gives students a chance to give something back to the many people who support them daily. (5) For example, students might learn about medicine and about how hospitals work by volunteering in a local emergency room. (6) It also provides a way for students to learn new things and have new educational experiences.

(7) Some educators argue that students, are too overloaded. (8) to take on any additional requirements (9) Since a community service program might require 100 hours of service in a year, some say it would take students away from homework and other important obligations. (10) Some people think Wilson High is overcrowded with students. (11) Still others say it's important for students to choose for themselves how and when they would like to contribute to society.

(12) Despite some educators' concerns about mandatory community service, I believe it's a terrific idea that benefits all. (13) It might add more balls to juggle in our busy daily lives, but we need to learn how to manage our time and how to fit in what's important. (14) And helping others is important. (15) If Wilson High does not adopt manditory community service, we'll be cheating not only our students' but our community as well.

DIRECTIONS
Use the passage on the previous page to answer the questions below. Circle the letter beside the correct answer.

1. What is the correct way to rewrite sentence 1?

    A. "Its better to give than to receive."

    B. "It's better to give than to recieve."

    C. "It's better to give than to receive."

    D. "Its better to give than two receive."

2. Where does sentence 5 belong?

    A. after sentence 3

    B. after sentence 6

    C. after sentence 8

    D. It is correct where it is.

3. Which sentence does NOT belong in the third paragraph?

    A. sentence 7

    B. sentence 8

    C. sentence 9

    D. sentence 10

4. What is the BEST way to combine sentences 7 and 8 and fix the errors?

    A. Some educators argue that students are too overloaded to take on any additional requirements.

    B. Some educators argue that students are too overloaded to take on any additional requirements

    C. Some educators argue. That students are too overloaded to take on any additional requirements.

    D. Some educators argue, that students are too overloaded to take on any additional requirements.

5. Which two words are incorrect in sentence 15?

    A. *community* and *cheating*

    B. *adopt* and *service*

    C. *manditory* and *students'*

    D. *Wilson* and *we'll*

DIRECTIONS
Now use what you have learned to revise and edit the draft of your speech on page 124. Write your revision on a separate sheet of paper. Pay attention to your focus, organization, and the clarity of your argument. Edit your draft for errors in spelling, punctuation, capitalization, grammar, and sentence structure.

DIRECTIONS
Read the following prompt and write a persuasive letter to your school newspaper.

In recent years, many school districts around the country have banned soft drinks and sugary snacks from high school vending machines. Some educators argue that soft drinks and sweet snacks at school are key factors in rising obesity rates among students. They believe only fruit juice, milk, and healthy snacks, like nuts and granola, should be stocked in school vending machines. Others believe students benefit from a choice of beverages and snacks. Opponents of banning soft drinks and sugary snacks say it is up to the students to make healthy choices for themselves.

In your opinion, should schools be allowed to provide soft drinks and sugary snacks in vending machines? Write a letter to your school newspaper stating your position on this issue and why you think the way you do.

On separate sheets of paper, write a draft of your letter. Then write a revised and edited version of your letter.

As you revise and edit, use this checklist:

- [ ] Do I take one position and state it clearly in my opener?
- [ ] Does my opener capture my readers' attention?
- [ ] Do I stay focused throughout the letter on the issue of sodas and snacks in school vending machines?
- [ ] Do I organize all of my points in a logical order?
- [ ] Do I give reasons, examples, and details to support my points?
- [ ] Do I think about counter-arguments and address them?
- [ ] Do I have a strong closing that sums up my position clearly?
- [ ] Do I stay focused on the purpose of my letter?
- [ ] Do I use correct spelling, punctuation, capitalization, and grammar?
- [ ] Do I use complete sentences?
- [ ] Do I vary my sentence lengths to make them interesting to the reader?

Lesson 10 • Informational Writing

Prewriting

The purpose of **informational writing** is to inform the reader or explain something. The writer states a main idea about the topic in a **thesis** statement and uses the rest of the composition to expand or explain that idea. The writer uses examples and facts to support the main idea. Types of informational writing include research papers, book and movie reviews, newspaper articles, travel guides, how-to guides, letters, and essays.

When writing an informational composition, remember to do the following:

- State the main idea of your composition early in the piece in a thesis statement.
- Identify several supporting points that you will explain in the body of your piece.
- Organize your ideas and points in a logical order.
- Include facts that are generally accepted to be true.
- Provide details that make general ideas more specific.
- Use explanations or examples to support your ideas.
- Provide appropriate materials such as maps, graphics, and definitions of terms when helpful.
- Assume the reader knows nothing about your topic. Provide enough information to fully explain your main idea and supporting details in a way that anyone could understand.
- End with a strong closing. It should wrap up the main idea of your composition.
- Use correct spelling, punctuation, capitalization, grammar, and sentence structure.

Brainstorming

Most young people have some responsibilities that require them to follow certain steps. For example, some young people have to clean their bedrooms each week. Imagine you are trying to explain a regular responsibility you have to a student from another country. What is the main idea you would convey about this responsibility? What information would you include? What examples or explanations might be needed?

Brainstorming will help you come up with ideas for an informational piece. List ideas for an informational piece on the next page.

1. IDEA _____

_____

2. IDEA _____

_____

3. IDEA _____

_____

4. IDEA _____

_____

Building Ideas

You have generated several ideas for an informational piece. Now build on your ideas by adding more thoughts and details. Choose your two best ideas from above. For each idea, think of the main idea you would convey and write it below. Then think of the different facts, examples, or details you would provide to support your main idea.

Idea 1: _____

Supporting facts, examples, or details:

    1. _____

    2. _____

    3. _____

    4. _____

Idea 2: _____

Supporting facts, examples, or details:

    1. _____

    2. _____

    3. _____

    4. _____

Organizing Your Informational Piece

In any informational writing, the ideas should be clear and easy to follow. They should flow logically from one point to the next. You can organize informational writing in:

- chronological order—put events in the order in which they happen
- logical order—group related ideas together
- order of importance—move from most important points to least (or the reverse)

DIRECTIONS
Pick one of your ideas from the previous page to write an informational piece. Use this graphic organizer to help plan out the structure.

Outline

Main point:

A. Subpoint: _____

    1. _____

    2. _____

B. Subpoint: _____

    1. _____

    2. _____

C. Subpoint: _____

    1. _____

    2. _____

Drafting

Openings

A strong **opening** draws the reader into your informational piece. It leaves the reader interested in finding out more. When you write an informational composition, it is important to state the main idea clearly in the opening. This will help readers follow the information or explanation and decide how well you convey this information throughout the composition.

As you prepare to write a draft of an informational piece, review these strategies for writing an effective opener:

Strategy	Example
State an attention-getting fact.	For more than twenty years, my mother has spent every Saturday morning cleaning our bathroom.
Use a personal example.	I walked into the kitchen and my eyes widened. The dishes in the sink were no longer a mound; they were a mountain. It was my job to reach the summit.
Introduce a definition.	The word *scouring* means more than simply cleaning the surface of something. Scouring means to clean fully, to remove through deep scrubbing, or to vigorously wash.
Include a famous quote.	"Give me liberty or give me death!" These words of Patrick Henry held great meaning when they were spoken in the tumultuous year of 1775. But many citizens still hold to Henry's ideas.
Make a broad, interesting statement about the topic.	Even in prehistoric times—before the invention of fancy cleaning products and devices—people have valued personal cleanliness.

DIRECTIONS
A student wrote an informational piece about China's first empire. The student explains how the first empire developed, who the leaders were, and how it ended. Evaluate his opening and write a stronger opening below. Review the strategies above as you write.

So, China had several different kingdoms and states. The kingdoms often fought each other. One leader united the various kingdoms to become one empire.

_____

_____

_____

_____

Transitions

Transitions signal the relationship between ideas in writing. They connect new ideas to the ideas that came before them. In informational writing, a writer shows cause and effect with words like *as a result, because, so,* and *therefore.* The writer shows contrasting ideas with words like *but, however,* and *in fact.* To make comparisons, writers use transitions such as *like, as well as,* or *similarly.* Words such as *after, before, finally, first,* and *then* show time. Other words like *above, beyond, here, on,* and *under* show place.

DIRECTIONS
Read this student's informational piece on the causes of the French Revolution. Choose the best transition words from the box below to complete her paper.

in fact	like	then	so
as a result	after	first	finally

Causes of the French Revolution

"Let them eat cake!" Legend has it that Marie Antoinette, the Queen of France, spoke these words about the suffering French people during the French Revolution. (1) _____, she never spoke these unfeeling words. (2) _____ many political conflicts, the French Revolution was more complicated than it is often portrayed. Some of the less glamorous causes of the French Revolution include long-standing poverty, failures in agricultural harvest, and high taxes for the peasants.

(3) _____, much of the peasantry was impoverished because of wars that had begun long before Louis XVI was king. Some of the wars began as early as 1740, but Louis XVI did not become king until 1774. (4) _____, King Louis the XVI inherited an unhappy populace.

(5) _____ a series of bad harvests depleted available food in the country. The food that did exist was very expensive, (6) _____ the people with the fewest resources were often near starving. Hungry families, with no hope of a future, became angry at the aristocracy that dominated them.

(7) _____, the peasants were burdened by heavy taxation. Feudal lords forced the peasants who lived on their land to pay more than they could. When the peasants could not pay their taxes, the lords took everything they had.

(8) _____ many years of simmering anger and frustration, the lower and middle classes revolted against the upper classes in a revolution that ended with the formation of the French Republic in 1792. Both Louis XVI and his wife Marie Antoinette were executed in 1793. However, unlike after the American Revolution, many more difficult years were ahead for France.

Closings

The **closing** of any composition is the final thought the writer leaves a reader. A strong closing in an informational piece summarizes the information conveyed in the piece. It might also give the reader something to think about in the future or make a connection with something the reader already knows about. Most importantly, the closing should follow logically from the rest of the piece.

As you prepare to write a draft of an informational piece, review these strategies for writing an effective closing:

Strategy	Example
Sum up the main idea.	After many years of simmering anger and frustration, the lower and middle classes revolted against the upper classes in a revolution that ended with the formation of the French Republic in 1792.
Make a more general statement about the topic.	Young people can learn a lot from studying the growth cycle of trees.
Explain that a process was completed.	At last, the washing machine completes spinning. I can place the clothes in the dryer, turn it on, and relax. What an exhausting day of work!
Spark your readers' imaginations.	Who knows what might have happened if the island of Japan had been open to the outside world earlier. We'll never know.

DIRECTIONS
A student wrote a short article about a trip he took to the Museum of Science and Industry in Chicago. He explained the features of the museum. Evaluate his closing and write a stronger closing below. Review the strategies above as you write.

So, like I said several times in the article, the Museum of Science and Industry is a pretty good place. And I saw a lot of interesting things to do there. I wonder if my brother might like to go visit it sometime. But maybe I didn't see all of it. Or maybe I only liked it because I was in a good mood that day.

_____

_____

_____

_____

_____

Drafting

You have generated ideas and reviewed openings, transitions, and closings. Now it is time to write a draft. A **draft** is a chance to get all of your ideas on paper and organize your composition. In writing an informational piece, remember to clearly state your main idea and write out each piece of support. Use specific examples, explanations, facts, details, and definitions. Write a strong closing. In drafting any informational piece, make sure to stay focused on the topic and keep your ideas organized logically.

DIRECTIONS
Use your notes from pages 129 and 130 and what you have learned about openings, transitions, and closings to write a draft of an informational piece. Begin your draft here and continue on a separate sheet of paper if necessary.

Title of Composition: _____

_____

_____

_____

_____

_____

_____

_____

_____

_____

_____

_____

_____

_____

_____

_____

_____

Step 3

Revising and Editing

Once you have written your first draft, you will need to **revise** and **edit.** In the revision process, a writer makes changes to improve his or her composition. Writers review the organization and focus of their draft, and how their ideas are supported. They watch for ways to make their writing more clear. Writers also make edits to correct mistakes in spelling, punctuation, capitalization, grammar, and sentence structure.

DIRECTIONS
Read these paragraphs from a student's informational article about bluegrass music. Look for ways to improve it, and answer the questions on the following page.

Bluegrass Music

(1) Until recently, I assumed that bluegrass music was a thing of the past. (2) It was something my uncle riley listened to but that was all. (3) I also thought that anyone who enjoyed or played bluegrass music lived deep in the southern part of the United States. (4) But not long ago, I discovered how wrong I was. (5) Not only is bluegrass music enjoying a popular comeback, but people all over the world enjoy the earthy melodies.

(6) Bluegrass music can be characterized by numerous vocal harmonies and purely acoustic sounds. (7) I found out my Grandma once played in a bluegrass band. (8) Often the instruments include guitar, banjo, mandolin, and stand-up bass. (9) The blending harmonic sounds are one reason that people appreciate the music.

(10) Another reason people like bluegrass music is it's abulity to create a melancholic sound. (11) Some people believe that nothing conveys a heartsick soul like a good bluegrass song. (12) However, bluegrass can also have uplifting melodies that set the feet to dancing. (13) In fact, many bluegrass musicians can strum their instruments with amazing speed.

(14) Todays bluegrass fans can be found across the globe. (15) Although most people still believe the best bluegrass bands are from the american south. (16) For example, did you see the movie *O Brother, Where Art Thou?* (17) You may think you are unfamiliar with bluegrass music, but you probably have heard more of it than you think. (18) If so, and if you enjoyed that music, you may be on your way to becoming a bluegrass fan yourself!

DIRECTIONS
Use the passage on the previous page to answer the questions below. Circle the letter beside the correct answer.

1. What is the correct way to rewrite sentence 2?

   A. It was something my uncle Riley listened to but that was all.

   B. It was something my Uncle riley listened to, but that was all.

   C. It was something my Uncle Riley listened to, but that was all.

   D. It was something my Uncle Riley listened to; but that was all.

2. Which sentence does NOT belong in the second paragraph?

   A. sentence 6

   B. sentence 7

   C. sentence 8

   D. sentence 9

3. Which two words are incorrect in sentence 10?

   A. *it's* and *abulity*

   B. *reason* and *music*

   C. *are* and *create*

   D. *melancholic* and *sound*

4. Where does sentence 16 belong?

   A. after sentence 14

   B. after sentence 17

   C. after sentence 18

   D. It is correct where it is.

5. What is the BEST way to combine sentences 14 and 15 and fix the errors?

   A. Today's bluegrass fan's can be found across the globe; although most people still believe the best bluegrass bands are from the american south.

   B. Today's bluegrass fans can be found across the globe, although most people still believe the best bluegrass bands are from the American south.

   C. Todays bluegrass fans can be found across the globe. Most people still believe the best bluegrass bands are from the american South.

   D. Today's bluegrass fans can be found across the globe although most people still believe the best bluegrass bands are from the american south.

DIRECTIONS
Now use what you have learned to revise and edit the draft of your informational piece on page 134. Write your revision on a separate sheet of paper. Pay attention to your focus, organization, and the clarity of the information you present. Edit your draft for errors in spelling, punctuation, capitalization, grammar, and sentence structure.

DIRECTIONS
Read the following prompt and write an informational essay for a community group you are in.

Role models are people that you admire because of the things they do or the way they behave. Perhaps you admire a role model for making personal sacrifices for someone else's benefit. Or maybe you admire a role model for working hard to reach a personal goal. A role model might be someone in your family, school, or community. You do not have to know someone personally to consider him or her a role model.

Who is your role model? Write an informational piece in which you identify your role model and explain why this person has played an important role in your life. Be sure to use details, examples, explanations, or definitions to support your main idea.

On separate sheets of paper, write a draft of your composition. Then write a revised and edited version of your composition.

As you revise and edit, use this checklist:

- ☐ Do I identify my role model in a thesis statement?

- ☐ Does my opener capture my readers' attention?

- ☐ Do I stay on the topic throughout the whole composition?

- ☐ Do I organize all of my points in a logical order?

- ☐ Do I give details, examples, explanations, and definitions to support my points?

- ☐ Do I have a strong closing that sums up my main idea clearly?

- ☐ Do I stay focused on the purpose of my composition?

- ☐ Do I use correct spelling, punctuation, capitalization, and grammar?

- ☐ Do I use complete sentences?

- ☐ Do I vary my sentence lengths to make them interesting to the reader?

Lesson 11 • Narrative Writing

Prewriting

Narrative writing tells readers a story or an account of something that has happened, whether real or fictional. The writer creates characters, a setting, a plot or series of events which include a problem and a solution, and a theme or message. Types of narrative writing include biography, memoir, autobiography, and fiction.

When writing a narrative composition, remember to do the following:

- Introduce and develop main and supporting characters through their dialogue, actions, movements, gestures, and expressions.

- Develop a setting for the story, including location, time, and environment that might affect the characters.

- Establish the main **conflict**, or problem, faced by characters in the story.

- Provide rising action that develops the tension of the story's main conflict.

- Include a **climax**, or turning point, in the story.

- Resolve the conflict in the story.

- Use descriptive, sensory details to create characters and setting.

- Use character, plot, and setting to convey your overall message.

- Use vivid verbs to illustrate action.

- Maintain consistent voice and point of view.

- Organize your events and ideas in a logical order. In narrative writing, events are often presented in chronological order.

- Use correct spelling, punctuation, capitalization, grammar, and sentence structure.

Brainstorming

Everyone has to work hard sometimes. Imagine a character your age who works hard and faces some specific challenges. What might your character be like? Where would your story take place? What problems might the character face? How would those problems be solved?

Brainstorming will help you come up with ideas for your narrative writing. List ideas for a narrative on the next page.

1. IDEA _____

2. IDEA _____

3. IDEA _____

4. IDEA _____

Building Ideas

You have generated several ideas for your narrative. Now build on your ideas by adding more thoughts and details. Choose your favorite idea from above. Then think of specific details for character, setting, and plot.

Idea: _____

Character:

    1. _____

    2. _____

Setting:

    1. _____

    2. _____

Plot:

    1. _____

    2. _____

Connecting Your Ideas

In any narrative, the events of the plot should be easy to follow. The central conflict should be clear and the rest of the story should revolve around it. The plot includes the events leading up to and following the climax.

DIRECTIONS:
Think about your idea for a narrative on page 139. Use this graphic organizer to help plot out the story.

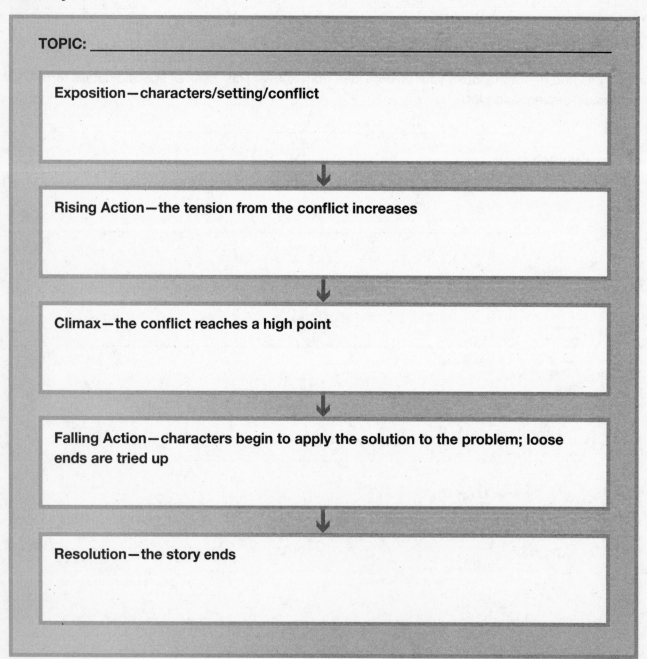

TOPIC: _____

Exposition—characters/setting/conflict

Rising Action—the tension from the conflict increases

Climax—the conflict reaches a high point

Falling Action—characters begin to apply the solution to the problem; loose ends are tried up

Resolution—the story ends

Drafting

Openings

A strong story **opening** captures the audience's attention and interest. When you write a narrative, it is important that readers want to follow the action and characters.

As you prepare to write a draft of a narrative, review these strategies for writing an effective opener:

Strategy	Example
Begin in the middle of action.	The flames shot more than 100 feet into the sky, and the crackling and falling wood roared as it fell to the ground.
Introduce characters with specific details.	The young boy bounded across the yard, his blond hair flying and his cheerful grin beaming. This wasn't unusual behavior for Jerome, the most genial kid on the entire block.
Introduce the setting by including interesting details.	The dark forest was silent and chilly. Not a soul walked across the needle-covered floor of the forest. Why should they? It was 1774 and a war was raging nearby. If anyone were in that forest, he or she would not want to be discovered.
Ask a question.	What is this place? How did I get here?
Use dialogue.	"I don't like this one bit," Mario said to his brother Ralph.

DIRECTIONS
A student wrote a narrative about a young boy who often got into trouble without meaning to. Evaluate the student's opening and write a stronger opening below. Review the strategies above as you write.

The boy was a kid who was pretty normal. But he sometimes got into trouble. He lived in a house on the corner. He walked to school each morning and home each afternoon. Other children in the neighborhood talked to him sometimes.

_____

_____

_____

_____

_____

Transitions

Smooth **transitions** lead the reader from one point to the next. They connect new ideas or events to the ideas or events that came before them. In narrative writing, a writer adds new events with transition words that show time order or sequence, such as: *then, next, immediately, in the meantime, already, now, when,* and *suddenly.* The writer shows contrasting ideas with words like *but* and *however.*

DIRECTIONS
Read this student's narrative. Choose the best transition words from the box below to complete her narrative.

suddenly	however	when	often
then	after	during	now

What It Means To Be a Winner

How could she get up that morning and face her life again? Would she be able to shake off yesterday's events?

(1) _____ her alarm clock blared loudly on Tuesday morning, Leah woke up to all these questions. Flopping over on her side, she curled herself into a tight ball and waited.

"Leah, it's time to get up, sweetheart," her mother spoke softly as she entered the room.

Leah did not move or speak. Her mother shuffled over in her slippers and sat down on Leah's bed. (2) _____ she switched on the light and looked around.

"I'd be feeling blue in a room this messy, too," her mom said, chuckling to herself.

(3) _____ Leah's room reflected her moods.

The room was a disaster. The contents of Leah's backpack had exploded onto the floor. In one corner, dirty jeans, crumpled jackets, and week-old t-shirts lay in a heap.

"(4) _____ what happened yesterday, Leah, I think you would be proud of yourself. Why do you seem upset (5) _____?"

"Proud?!" Leah leaped right out of her bed, knocking several books onto the floor, "Why should I be proud? I beat my best friend in the state tennis tournament! Marianne probably spent all last night sobbing in her bed!"

(6) _____ the expression on her mother's face changed. (7) _____ the silence, Leah glanced over at her mother, who was wiping away a tear.

"I had not even thought of it that way, Leah. You have the most generous heart I know. Last night I went to bed thinking how proud I was of you for winning the tournament. I never stopped to think about how Marianne might be feeling about losing. I'm so pleased you won; (8) _____, I'm more proud of your compassionate heart than I am of your tennis skills."

She leaned over and embraced Leah warmly.

"But," she continued, "you'll probably be glad to know that Marianne called early this morning to congratulate you."

Closings

The closing, or **denouement**, in narrative writing is the story's resolution. The closing is the last chance to make an impression or convey an action. A strong closing in a narrative piece tells important final events or describes the emotions of characters as the story ends. It might also emphasize the theme of the narrative. Most importantly, the closing should follow logically from the rest of the piece.

As you prepare to write a draft of a narrative piece, review these strategies for writing an effective closing:

Strategy	Example
Make a wrap-up statement about the setting.	The logs crackled in the fire, and the dogs gradually wandered into the sitting room. As dusk fell, the room became one of peace and safety.
Provide final character details.	Charlotte looked out the window and realized that she would always live in this house and be happy there.
Make a theme statement.	That is what friendship is really about, after all: seeking the good of someone else even when it does not benefit yourself.
Use a character quote.	"It is a far, far better thing that I do, than I have ever done; it is a far, far better rest that I go to than I have ever known." —*A Tale of Two Cities,* by Charles Dickens
Use a wrap-up question.	And could anyone argue that Colleen had finally found what she had been looking for?

DIRECTIONS
A student wrote a narrative about an ancient monk who spread wisdom through his travels. Evaluate his closing and write a stronger closing below. Review the strategies above as you write.

So then the monk just stopped traveling. People still liked him, I guess, but he was getting older. Sometimes he felt pretty strong, but other days he was just too tired to move around. I'm pretty sure people still came to him for advice and comfort, but he really had to stick around his own house for the rest of his life.

_____

_____

_____

_____

_____

Drafting

You have generated ideas and reviewed openings, transitions, and closings. Now it is time to write a draft. A **draft** is a chance to get all of your ideas on paper and organize your composition. In writing a narrative draft, remember to introduce the key elements—setting, character, and plot. Develop each of these elements through descriptive detail, dialogue, and action. In drafting any narrative piece, make sure to stay focused on the final outcome. All the details in the piece should lead to the resolution.

DIRECTIONS
Use your notes from pages 139 and 140 and what you have learned about openings, transitions, and closings to write a draft of a narrative piece. Begin your draft here and continue on a separate sheet of paper if necessary.

Title of Narrative: _____

_____

_____

_____

_____

_____

_____

_____

_____

_____

_____

_____

_____

_____

Step 3

Revising and Editing

Once you have written your first draft, you will need to **revise** and **edit.** In the revision process, a writer makes changes to improve his or her composition. Writers review the organization and focus of their draft, and how their ideas are supported. They watch for ways to make their writing more clear. Writers also make edits to correct mistakes in spelling, punctuation, capitalization, grammar, and sentence structure.

DIRECTIONS
Read these paragraphs from a student's narrative. Look for ways to improve it, and answer the questions on the following page.

Brotherly Love

(1) Even if I live to be a hundred years old, I'll never forget the day my big brother stood up for me after school.

(2) My brother is a veteran twelfth grader. (3) I were a brand knew ninth grader. (4) At times, I even wondered if I embarrassed him. (5) Peter had always been a fair brother to me, even when we were very young. (6) But as he got older, I often wondered how interested he was in his younger sister.

(7) But this school day changed everything. (8) As usual, we had gotten out of school on time and were meeting up to walk home. (9) Our father had requested that we come home right away to help pack the car for a weekend trip. (10) My favorite travel snack has always been trail mix.

(11) As I crossed the schoolyard toward my brother, several other students called out criticisms of my brilliant red hat. (12) The phrase I heard most was "tomato-head."

(13) These students has offended my brother on too accounts. (14) First of all, my grandmother, who had died the previous summer, had knit that hat. (15) She had worked hard at it, even when her eyesight had begun to fail. (16) My brother loved my grandmother with devoted affection. (17) Second, that hat was on *my* head, and my brother had no time for anyone mocking his sister.

(18) Leaping across the yard to my rescue, my brother stood tall and strong. (19) Speaking loudly, but respectfully, he put his arm around me and said, "For your information, that hat represents the two women I love most in this world. (20) I suggest you never bring it up again."

(21) Peter's words still comfort me. (22) When I feel alone or disdressed, I think of Peters' brave assertion of his love for me, and I am reminded of the value of family.

DIRECTIONS
Use the passage on the previous page to answer the questions below. Circle the letter beside the correct answer.

1. What is the BEST way to combine sentences 2 and 3 and fix the errors?

   A. My brother is a veteran twelfth grader I am a brand-new ninth grader.

   B. My brother, a veteran twelfth grader, and I was a brand-new ninth grader.

   C. My brother and I were veteran twelfth graders and ninth graders.

   D. My brother was a veteran twelfth grader, and I was a brand-new ninth grader.

2. Where does sentence 4 belong?

   A. after sentence 5

   B. after sentence 6

   C. after sentence 7

   D. It is correct where it is.

3. Which sentence does NOT belong in the third paragraph?

   A. sentence 7

   B. sentence 8

   C. sentence 9

   D. sentence 10

4. What is the correct way to rewrite sentence 13?

   A. These students are offending my brother on too accounts.

   B. The student have offended my brother on to accounts.

   C. These students had offended my brother on two accounts.

   D. It is correct as is.

5. Which two words are incorrect in sentence 22?

   A. *alone* and *brave*

   B. *assertion* and *begin*

   C. *disdressed* and *Peters'*

   D. *reminded* and *value*

DIRECTIONS
Now use what you have learned to revise and edit the draft of your narrative on page 144. Write your revision on a separate sheet of paper. Pay attention to the details of your characters, setting, and plot. Edit your draft for errors in spelling, punctuation, capitalization, grammar, and sentence structure.

DIRECTIONS
Read the following prompt and write a narrative piece.

Surprises can be both positive and negative. A good surprise can change your day—or even your life. A negative surprise can be anything from a small discouragement to a real tragedy.

Write a narrative piece about a character who encounters a surprise.

On separate sheets of paper, write a draft of your story. Then write a revised and edited version of your story.

As you revise and edit, use this checklist:

☐ Does my opener capture my readers' attention?

☐ Do I introduce my characters and setting early in the story?

☐ Do I clearly establish the conflict and develop it with rising action?

☐ Do I use descriptive and sensory detail to create the setting and characters?

☐ Do the dialogue, action, and expressions of characters make them more alive for the reader?

☐ Do I include a climax where the conflict reaches a turning point?

☐ Do I use characters, setting, and plot to convey my main message?

☐ Do I use vivid verbs to illustrate action?

☐ Do I organize all of my events in a logical order?

☐ Do I have a strong closing that provides resolution of the story?

☐ Do I use correct spelling, punctuation, capitalization, and grammar?

☐ Do I use complete sentences?

☐ Do I vary my sentence lengths to make them interesting to the reader?

Lesson 12 • Literary Writing

Prewriting

In **expressive writing**, a writer explores his or her own ideas through personal writing such as memoir, fiction, drama, or poetry. A writer may also use expressive writing to convey an opinion about a piece of literature.

In a **literary response**, the writer's purpose is to convey his or her interpretation of a piece of literature. The writer examines various elements of the text—characters, action, themes, setting, and literary devices—and draws conclusions about the overall meaning. The writer uses examples from the text to support his or her interpretation. Literary response may be written for fiction, nonfiction, drama, and poetry.

When writing a literary response, remember to do the following:

- Read the literary text carefully.
- Interpret some aspect of the text; for example: characters and their actions, the importance of the setting, or the point of view in the text.
- Identify and interpret symbolism, metaphors, and other literary devices.
- State your interpretation clearly in the thesis of your literary response.
- Organize your interpretation around a **thesis** statement.
- Support your thesis statement with evidence from the text.
- Conclude your literary response by restating your interpretation and basic points.
- Use correct spelling, punctuation, capitalization, grammar, and sentence structure.

Brainstorming

You read literature regularly for school and pleasure. Think about some of the short stories, novels, poems, or plays you have read recently. What interpretations might you make about several of them? Why do some of them seem to be so interesting? Does a certain character stand out in your mind as especially well-developed?

Brainstorming will help you come up with ideas for a literary response. List ideas for a piece of literature you might like to respond on the next page.

1. IDEA _____

   _____

2. IDEA _____

   _____

3. IDEA _____

   _____

4. IDEA _____

   _____

Building Ideas

You have generated several ideas for a literary response. Now build on your ideas by adding more thoughts and details. Choose your two best ideas from above. For each idea, think of the interpretation you would make and write it below. Then think of the different points you would make to support your interpretation.

Interpretation 1: _____

Supporting points:

    1. _____

    2. _____

    3. _____

    4. _____

Interpretation 2: _____

Supporting points:

    1. _____

    2. _____

    3. _____

    4. _____

Connecting Your Ideas

In any literary response, the ideas should be easy to follow. They should flow logically from one to the next. Each point of the writer's interpretation should be supported with specific examples from the text. No points should be weak, vague, or off the topic.

DIRECTIONS

Pick one of your ideas from the previous page to write a literary response. Use this graphic organizer to help plan the structure.

Analyzing a Piece of Literature

Interpretation	Supporting examples from the story: (possible elements: character, setting, plot events, point of view, theme, or literary devices)

Step 2

Drafting

Openings

A strong **opening** captures the audience's attention and interest. When you write a literary response, it is important to state your interpretation clearly in your opening. This will help readers follow your interpretation and decide how well you support your point of view throughout.

As you prepare to write a draft of a literary response, review these strategies for writing an effective opener:

Strategy	Example
Make an early reference to the literary text.	When Edgar Allan Poe writes "The Raven," he writes about far more than a dark bird on a dark night. He uses imagery that conveys the darkness in the human soul.
Give background information to the literary work.	Harper Lee, the author of *To Kill a Mockingbird,* grew up in a world similar to her main character in her famous novel. It is this personal angle that makes the novel resonate with such richness.
Ask a question that directs your reader to your main idea.	What would cause a young boy to abandon his mother and his home to seek adventure on the high seas? Only a youngster with nothing to lose would potentially throw his life away in this manner.
Use a definition to connect to the main idea.	Technically, companionship is defined as a relationship of fellowship or of common feeling. But the story *Huckleberry Finn* redefines what true companionship really is.

DIRECTIONS
A student wrote a literary response to a short story he had read. This student thought that one of the minor characters set the tone for the whole book. Evaluate his opening and write a stronger opening below. Review the strategies above as you write.

There is a guy in this book that doesn't show up that often. Sometimes he pops up, but he is not a major character. But he has a lot to say, and what he does say, is very important. I like this character a lot, and I think he is more important than he may seem to the story.

_____

_____

_____

_____

_____

Transitions

Smooth **transitions** lead the reader from one point to the next. They connect new ideas to the ideas that came before them. In literary writing, a writer adds new ideas with transition words like *as well as, for example*, and *in particular*. The writer shows similarities with words like *both, similarly*, and *likewise*. Contrasting ideas are presented with words like *in comparison, on the contrary, unlike, although*, and *however*. He or she concludes or sums up a line of reasoning with words such as *finally, on the whole,* and *to sum up*.

DIRECTIONS
Read this student's literary response to Robert Frost's poem "Mending Wall." Choose the best transition words from the box below to complete her essay.

in the end	unlike	therefore	however
but	both	in contrast	for example

"Mending Wall"

In Robert Frost's poem "Mending Wall," the reader learns of two neighbors who share a wall that divides their property. (1) _____, they do not share the same view of that wall. The poem's speaker sees the wall as an unnecessary division, while his neighbor believes that the wall is important in keeping boundaries.

(2) _____ the speaker and the neighbor own and care for their adjoining properties. They meet in spring time to repair any damage that was done during the last winter. (3) _____ the speaker realizes that the wall is not really doing much good for their boundary. (4) _____, there are no cows that will cross over into the other man's property. Nor will the apple trees ever cross over and eat the other man's pine cones. Practically speaking, the wall is somewhat pointless.

(5) _____, the neighbor believes that "good fences make good neighbors." He wants the wall to be rebuilt as strong as ever. (6) _____ the speaker, the neighbor cannot think beyond the tradition of keeping fences between people. This barrier is more than a physical barrier. It is a psychological barrier, as well, which prevents the men from become more than polite neighbors. (7) _____, the speaker recognizes that he and the neighbor will never be true friends.

(8) _____, the speaker has come to a new understanding, but the neighbor will continue in his traditional way of living. Because his father and grandfather before him built walls, this man will also build walls—both physical and metaphorical.

Closings

The **closing** of any composition is the final thought the writer leaves a reader. The closing is the last chance to make an impression or get a message across. A strong closing in a literary response restates the main interpretation and the basic supporting points. It might also repeat important terms or suggest larger implications of the interpretation. Most importantly, the closing should follow logically from the rest of the piece.

As you prepare to write a draft of a persuasive piece, review these strategies for writing an effective closing:

Strategy	Example
Sum up your interpretation.	Sara Beth's compassionate language, her steady kindness to her mother, and her attitude towards her difficult situation show that she, more than any other character, has true virtue.
Use a quotation that speaks to the overall theme.	This story shows how circumstances are rarely what they seem. As the noble Mr. Parker states early on: "Trust must be earned, and I do not believe Clarence has yet earned it."
Suggest further implications of the interpretation.	If Simeon is really the dark character he seems to be, what will the future hold for his wife and daughters? Although the novel stops short of these details, the reader can make certain guesses about what lies beyond the end of the novel.

DIRECTIONS
A student wrote a literary response to a novel about a family that lived in an isolated region of the country. She tied the personalities of the characters to the isolation they felt in their setting. Evaluate her closing and write a stronger closing below. Review the strategies above as you write.

As a conclusion, I think the mother was very isolated. The father was also isolated, as were the kids. All the characters were isolated, which showed up in their personalities. They lived in an isolated place, as my paper suggests, and they also became emotionally isolated. Maybe if they moved, they would be different.

_____

_____

_____

_____

_____

Drafting

You have generated ideas and reviewed openings, transitions, and closings. Now it is time to write a draft. A **draft** is a chance to get all of your ideas on paper and organize your composition. In writing a literary response, remember to clearly state your interpretation and write out each supporting point for your interpretation. Support each point with specific examples from the text, and write a strong closing. In drafting any literary response, make sure to stay focused on the topic.

DIRECTIONS

Use your notes from pages 149 and 150 and what you have learned about openings, transitions, and closings to write a draft of a literary response to a piece of literature. Begin your draft here and continue on a separate sheet of paper if necessary.

Title of Composition: _____

_____

_____

_____

_____

_____

_____

_____

_____

_____

_____

_____

_____

_____

_____

_____

Step 3

Revising and Editing

Once you have written your first draft, you will need to **revise** and **edit**. In the revision process, a writer makes changes to improve his or her composition. Writers review the organization and focus of their draft, and how their ideas are supported. They watch for ways to make their writing more clear. Writers also make edits to correct mistakes in spelling, punctuation, capitalization, grammar, and sentence structure.

DIRECTIONS
Read these paragraphs from a student's literary response to George Orwell's novel *Animal Farm*. Look for ways to improve it, and answer the questions on the following page.

Animal Farm

(1) What educated adult really believes in talking animals? (2) Perhaps none really believe, but that has not stopped the success of George Orwell's 1946 dystopian novel *Animal Farm*. (3) Of course, the novel is not really meant to depict a realistic picture of animals. (4) Most countries now have fewer farms than they did a hundred years ago. (5) Instead, it is a direct criticism of the Soviet government of the 1940s. (6) Although the novel points its finger at the corruption in the Soviet Union at the time, many of the criticisms also apply to current governments.

(7) There is little argument that the main intension of "Animal Farm" was the criticism of the Soviet Union. (8) Orwell was familiar with the corruption within communism, and he used his literary skills to create a "fairy tale" which creates a similar community within a farm.

(9) At the beginning of the novel, the animals overthrowed the humans. (10) They do this in order two develop there own Government. (11) By the end of the novel, the commandment has been changed to read: "All animals are equal, but some animals are more equal than others." (12) They originally intend their government to show equality to all animals. (13) In fact, one of their early commandments is "All animals are equal." (14) Eventually, however, the system begins to break down as the pigs try to take over the leadership.

(15) Orwell shows the danger of a leadership of one. (16) For example, the head pig in *Animal Farm* eventually oppresses the other animals on the farm, including sending a much-loved horse to an undeserved death. (17) He plays on the ignorance and trust of the general population to strengthen his own position.

(18) Although this criticizm was accurate about the Soviet Union, the author leaves readers to consider weather the same question applies to current societies. (19) Are there really any societies where all humans are treated equally? (20) Or do we in fact live in societies were some humans are more equal than others?

DIRECTIONS
Use the passage on the previous page to answer the questions below. Circle the letter beside the correct answer.

1. Which sentence does NOT belong in the first paragraph?

    A. sentence 2

    B. sentence 3

    C. sentence 4

    D. sentence 5

2. What is the correct way to rewrite sentence 7?

    A. There is little argument that the main intention of *Animal Farm* was the criticism of the Soviet Union.

    B. There are little argument that the main intension of "Animal Farm" were the criticism of the Soviet Union.

    C. There be little argument that the main intension of *Animal Farm* was the criticism of the Soviet Union.

    D. There is little argument that the main intention of *Animal Farm* was the criticism of the soviet union.

3. Where does sentence 11 belong?

    A. at the beginning of the paragraph

    B. after sentence 12

    C. after sentence 14

    D. It is correct where it is.

4. What is the BEST way to combine sentences 9 and 10 and fix the errors?

    A. The animals overthrow the humans they do this in order two develop there own Government.

    B. At the beginning of the novel, the animals overthrow the humans in order to develop their own government.

    C. The animals overthrow the humans at the beginning of the novel in order two develop there own Government.

    D. At the beginning of the novel, the animals overthrow the humans; they do this in order to develop there own government.

5. Which two words are incorrect in sentence 18?

    A. *accurate* and *author*

    B. *leaves* and *consider*

    C. *applies* and *societies*

    D. *criticizm* and *weather*

DIRECTIONS
Now use what you have learned to revise and edit the draft of your literary response on page 154. Write your revision on a separate sheet of paper. Pay attention to your focus, organization, and the clarity of your interpretation. Edit your draft for errors in spelling, punctuation, capitalization, grammar, and sentence structure.

DIRECTIONS
Read the following prompt and write an expressive poem.

People often associate memories with sensory details that help them to recall an incident. For example, a certain smell might be linked with a childhood memory of a trip to the zoo in springtime. These memories are often connected to strong emotions, as well.

Write a poem where you use sensory details to recall a memory that holds strong emotions for you.

On separate sheets of paper, write a draft of your own poem. Then write a revised and edited version of your poem.

As you revise and edit, use this checklist:

☐ Do I express strong emotions in the poem?

☐ Do I convey a personal memory?

☐ Do I make it clear that some of the ideas or feelings in the poem are universal?

☐ Do I use sensory details and descriptive language that shows rather than tells?

☐ Do I stay focused on the purpose of my poem?

☐ Do I use correct spelling, punctuation, capitalization, and grammar, as appropriate in a poem?

Glossary

adjective a word that describes a noun (Lessons 3, 5)

adverb a word that describes a verb, adjective, or another adverb (Lesson 5)

brainstorm think about and plan a piece of writing before beginning a first draft (Lessons 9, 10, 11, 12)

capitalization the use of upper case or capital letters (Lesson 3)

clause a group of words with a subject and a verb (Lesson 6)

climax the turning point in a story (Lesson 11)

closing the end or conclusion of a composition (Lessons 9, 10, 11, 12)

comparative adjective an adjective that compares two nouns by adding –er or using more (Lesson 5)

comparative adverb an adverb that compares two verbs by adding –er or using more (Lesson 5)

complex sentence a sentence with a dependent clause and an independent clause (Lesson 7)

compound sentence two or more simple sentences joined by a semicolon or a comma and a conjunction (Lesson 7)

compound-complex sentence a sentence that contains more than one main (or independent) clause and at least one dependent clause (Lesson 7)

conflict a problem in narrative writing (Lesson 11)

dangling or **misplaced modifier** a group of words that is not near the word or group of words it modifies (Lesson 8)

declarative sentence a sentence that makes a statement and ends with a period (Lesson 7)

denouement a story's resolution (Lesson 11)

dependent or **subordinate clause** a clause that cannot stand alone and must be attached to an independent clause (Lesson 6)

draft the first attempt at writing a

composition (Lessons 9, 10, 11, 12)

exclamatory sentence a sentence that expresses strong feelings and ends with an exclamation point (Lesson 7)

expressive writing writing that expresses an author's own ideas through personal writing such as memoir, fiction, drama, or poetry (Lesson 12)

gerund a verb that ends in –ing but acts as a noun (Lesson 8)

homophones words that sound alike but have different spellings and meanings (Lesson 1)

imperative sentence a sentence that gives a command or instruction and ends with a period (Lesson 7)

independent clause a clause that stands alone (Lesson 6)

infinitive the basic to form of a verb (Lesson 8)

informational writing writing that informs the reader or explains something (Lesson 10)

interrogative sentence a sentence that asks a question and ends with a question mark (Lesson 7)

literary response an interpretation of a piece of literature (Lesson 12)

narrative writing writing that tells a story (Lesson 11)

noun a person, place, thing, or idea (Lesson 5)

opening the start of a composition (Lessons 9, 10, 11, 12)

parallel structure sentence structure that expresses ideas equally; keeping similar parts of a sentence in the same form so that the reader can see that they form a connected list of words or phrases (Lesson 8)

participle a verb that ends in –ing, -ed, or –en but acts as an adjective or can modify the subject of a sentence (Lesson 8)

parts of speech nouns, verbs, adjectives, and

adverbs (Lesson 5)

persuasive writing writing meant to convince the readers to think a certain way or take a certain action (Lesson 9)

phrase a group of words that does not have a subject or a verb (Lesson 6)

plural more than one person or thing (Lesson 4)

predicate the part of a sentence that contains a verb that tells something about the subject (Lesson 6)

proper adjective a word that specifies or modifies a proper noun (Lesson 3)

proper noun a specific person, place, or thing that requires capitalization (Lessons 3, 5)

punctuation the use of marks that help a reader understand the meaning of a sentence (Lesson 2)

purpose a reason for writing (Lesson 9)

revise and edit to make changes to improve a composition (Lessons 9, 10, 11, 12)

run-on sentence two or more independent clauses joined incorrectly (Lesson 6)

sentence a complete thought that contains a subject, a predicate, and proper punctuation (Lesson 6)

sentence fragment an incomplete sentence that lacks either a subject or a verb (Lesson 6)

sentence structure how a sentence is put together (Lesson 8)

simple sentence an independent clause (Lesson 7)

singular one person or thing (Lesson 4)

spelling the accepted arrangement of letters in a word that makes written text easy to understand (Lesson 1)

subject the noun of a sentence that performs the action (Lessons 4, 6)

subject-verb agreement the relationship between a sentence's subject and its verb (Lesson 4)

superlative adjective an adjective that compares more than two nouns by adding –*est* or using *most* (Lesson 5)

superlative adverb an adverb that compares more than two verbs by adding -*est* or using *most* (Lesson 5)

thesis a sentence that expresses the main idea of a topic (Lessons 10, 12)

transition a word or phrase that leads readers from one idea to the next (Lessons 9, 10, 11, 12)

types of sentences different sentences with different purposes (Lesson 7)

verb a word that shows action or a state of being (Lesson 5)

NOTES